Practical Perspectives on Youth

Practical Perspectives on Youth

Engagement and Mobilisation Strategy

by

Odianose Dominic Matthew

ᴁ

Strategic Book Publishing and Rights Co.

Strategic Book Publishing and Rights Co.
12620 FM 1960, Suite A4-507
Houston, TX 77065
www.sbpra.com

ISBN: 978-1-61204-290-9

Dedication

This book is dedicated to all lovers of youth work and young people in the world fighting to have an identity.

Acknowledgements

Oliver Wendell Holmes once said, "What lies behind us and what lies before us are tiny matters compared to what lies within us." This book is all about what lies within, and my experiences working with young people: various interactions with youths across different divides, hands-on training in youth development, and volunteering activities I have been involved in for many years in the social sector.

In publishing this book, I have been helped by many who shared and trusted my vision for young people.

My gratitude goes to Mr. Emmanuel Ugwu, chief correspondent for *Thisday* newspaper in Abia, Nigeria, who took the pain, despite his tight schedule, to do the initial editorial work and critique for the book. I would also like to thank him for his editorial support throughout the course of this book.

My former director, Mr. Segun Adeniji, and my senior colleagues at the Youth Development Department of the Lagos State Ministry of Youth, Sports, and Social Development in Alausa, Lagos, also provided great support to me while I was writing this book. I indeed remain very grateful for his suggestions and moral support over the years when he was the head of the department.

My deepest appreciation also goes to Dr. Frank Akponsah for his editorial suggestions, feedback, and the time he invested going through my manuscript despite his busy schedule. I am indebted to him for the belief in my vision and seed offering he invested to ensure the book came out at this time. It is my prayer that he and his ministry receive a double portion in return for this singular act of love and generosity.

When you are alone in the cold, helpers come your way through destiny. Some of those who have contributed financially to the production of this book, to whom I am also grateful, are engineer Ibikunle S. Ogunbayo of KOA Consultants Ltd., Lagos, and Mr. Ifeanyi Onyibo of Radac Communications System, Ikeja, Lagos.

Even though we have our differences, my appreciation also goes to Mr. Andrew Bourdillon with his family and Ikechukwu Okonkwo for accommodating me while I was writing this book in 2008. I appreciate my siblings for their prayers and moral support. I'd also like to thank my mentor, Rev. Fr. Luke C. Nwamuo, of the Vincentian community, Enugu, for his support throughout my undergraduate days and his belief in me to this day. There are many others I may not be able to mention now, who have acted as a rock for me when it seemed like I was sinking into a valley of darkness.

My acknowledgements would not be complete if I failed to say how grateful I am to my online coaches Terry Whalin, Arielle Ford, and Dvorah Lansky for all their educational author webinars that have been inspiring eye openers for me. These webinars have enhanced my capacity in building this chosen career. Thank you all for sharing your challenges and successes in the writing world.

My sincere gratitude goes to Zuzana, my partner, for her moral and financial contributions to the production of this book when other pressures seemed to be weighing me down from my career focus.

And to my publishers, Strategic Book Publishing and Rights Agency, who still believed in my work despite all the time it took for me to finally progress with it. I appreciate every bit of editorial advice. Working with their team has opened another chapter in my career. My sincere thanks go to the editorial team, Bruce, Vicky, and the entire team who have worked with me on this project. Thank you also for hounding me with emails—otherwise I may not have sent it off. You rock.

Above all, I remain eternally grateful to God for sustaining me in this struggle and giving me the wisdom to continue to use my talent in imparting knowledge and helping in my own little way to shape our current generation of youths.

I thank all of you for your contributions, and may God reward your labour of love accordingly.

Contents

Endorsement for Practical Perspectives on Youth

This book is a must-read for every stakeholder in youth development. I recommend it to parents, guardians, teachers, clerics, social workers, and those involved in the administration of justice. It is the work of a man with undisguised interest in and consummate passion for youth development. Left for him no youth should be a delinquent. I see this book as a practical and timely contribution in the quest to safeguard the future generation and build a crime-free society.

—**Mr. Emmanuel Ugwu, chief correspondent,**
Thisday **newspaper, Umuahia, Abia State**

It is a well-researched work. Keep the flag flying.

—**Mr. Segun Adeniji, former director,**
Youth Development Department, Lagos
State Ministry of Youth, Sports, and Social
Development, Alausa, Lagos

It is well written and factual.

—**Dr. Frank Amponsah, senior lecturer,**
Middlesex University, London

It is a must-read for everyone with a burning desire for youth development.

—Mr. Dayo Israel, special assistant for international relations, strategy, and community development, National Assembly of Nigeria, Abuja

Foreword

Today more than ever, youth development, especially in Africa, needs to be at the forefront of government agenda. For many decades the cliché "youths are the leaders of tomorrow" has been sung into our ears. The time is now to make that cliché a reality and give young people a voice, give them a chance, and create an environment that enables them to excel.

Corruption continues to deepen within our society, and we have lost the values that our founding fathers cherished. There are hardly any icons to look up to. However, we are at a defining moment to save our future and stand up together against all the ills of our society, which jeopardize the future of our nation.

These, among other things, are what *Practical Perspectives on Youth*, an eight-chapter book written by Odianose Dominic Matthew, aim to expose and correct after thorough research into issues affecting this vulnerable social sector.

The book, a thoroughly researched book written in simplified English, covers various strategies of mobilization and working with young people to harness their talent for community and national development, how those who work with these youth organizations can network for success, and how the problems of youth crime and drug addiction can be reduced by applying a different approach.

The author's practical solutions proffered from a background of research and experience gained while working with young people in Lagos State are particularly commendable and an asset that qualifies him as an authority in the field.

This book is written out of Dominic's wish to fill a vacuum in the youth industry and a burning desire to promote change in the professional practice. Dominic has traveled to conferences far and wide whose primary focus was on social issues.

There is a growing and immediate need to focus on young people, especially in Nigeria, in the face of youth unrest and kidnapping in the Niger Delta region. Because of the high rates of unemployment and youth involvement in crime and drugs, the nation needs worthy leaders to take up the mantle tomorrow.

I congratulate Mr. Odianose Dominic Matthew, a determined, unassuming youth himself, on his singular effort to put these practical perspectives in black and white in this book so that it can become a reference for those who work with young minds. I shall not hesitate to recommend this book, filled with insight and pragmatic solutions to youth work, to all lovers of young people globally, social workers, students of social work in our higher institutions, youth organizations in churches, mosques, and nongovernmental organizations (NGOs) to read and apply its strategies. The youths will be the ultimate benefactors.

It's a must-read for everyone with a burning desire for youth development.

Dayo Israel, special assistant for international relations, strategy, and community development, National Assembly of Nigeria, Abuja

Introduction

When I was still a teenager, I came across two popular maxims: "You cannot judge the quality of a book by its cover" and "Knowledge is power." The actual meanings of these adages didn't sink in for me until I started buying books and reading them as if my life depended on them. Indeed, like Daniel in the Holy Bible, my transformation depended on it, and that gave me an edge in many instances over those who don't read or have stopped reading.

I also came to understand that there is nothing under the sun hidden in a book if only we can take the pain to seek out the book, read it, and apply its theories. It is little wonder that even the Holy Bible said, "My people will perish for lack of knowledge." There is also that popular saying, "He who does not read is no better than an illiterate." After conducting several researches into youth affairs over the years, both as a member and an active volunteer in some voluntary youth organizations, coupled with my exposure to social discourse at international conferences, I have come to realize that young people are the same everywhere, and they share one common identity: being youths.

I decided to write this book over five years ago, but I just couldn't find the time and space needed for such an exercise until 2007, when I travelled out of Nigeria. Before then I could not find the time to put the pieces together and form what you now have in your hands today: a step-by-step guide to youth mobilization and empowerment.

While I was writing this book, I had professionals such as social workers, health workers, students of social work, parents, church leaders, youth workers, and volunteers offer their advice and opinions regarding our youth. Whether you operate within a government institution, nongovernmental organization, or as a volunteer, as long you work with the youths, there is a need to emphasize and streamline the concept of youth. I am confident perspectives in this book will allow these people to efficiently and effectively harness the potential inherent in young people.

I do not, however, in any way suggest or create the impression of having the best solution to all youth problems, but I'm convinced that, by applying different strategies and dynamic approaches to problematic social issues, we can all deliver better results than we already have without undermining the existing structure.

The first chapter discusses the subject of youth identity and tries to resolve the misconceptions surrounding who and what a youth is.

Chapter 2 discusses the five strategies of mobilization and how youth workers or volunteers can harness the potential of young people for community and nation building.

In Chapter 3, networking as a means of achieving success in youth project formulation and execution, and the benefits attached to it when youth workers or volunteers are organizing development project networks, is discussed.

In Chapter 4, attempts were made to bring civic rights and obligations of the youths to the front burner, giving an historical perspective of how Nigerian youths have volunteered and how the enjoyment of their inalienable rights is dependent on them fulfilling their obligations to the state.

Chapter 5 centers on youth and crime. It exposes the contributing factors that lead youths to crime and how these can be reduced using practical initiatives.

Youth and HIV/AIDS are discussed in Chapter 6. Youths form the highest percentage of those carrying the virus. This is partly because youths exhibit risky behaviors that expose them to the virus; thus, it became expedient to broaden the research. Over the years, I have had the opportunity to speak with youths who are living positive lives in spite of contracting the disease, so I considered it necessary to add a voice to the struggle to reduce the increasing infection rate among our youths, particularly in Africa where it's still a taboo to discuss sexuality with young people, who form the bulk of those suffering from HIV. If that is not bad enough, hardly 10 percent of them can remember how they came in contact with the virus. The reason is not farfetched: Many of our youths are careless with their sexuality and their health, perilously ignoring the popular saying, "Health is wealth."

Chapter 7 exposes the factors behind why youths get involved in substance abuse and further discusses the effects and challenges of combating youth drug addiction, particularly in Africa, and how it can be reduced.

The last chapter focuses on how young people and the voluntary sector can tap into the financial market and increase their financial knowledge about the capital market and opportunities available to increase wealth by safely investing for tomorrow.

I believe this book is a must-have and collector's item for anybody who works and wants to succeed in managing the most vulnerable segment of our population: youths.

My view is not nurtured from the economic sense of it, but from my practice over the years, in which I have seen people trying to benefit as youths when they can no longer be counted as one, thereby preventing the younger ones from taking their rightful place. In addition, some laws and practice in management of the youths in Africa are not only outdated but will take the youths back to the traditional era when they were only seen but not heard. Government institutions and voluntary organizations also follow the outdated national youth development policy. Consequently, the private sector shies away from investing in most youth developmental projects that will benefit their target market, with few exceptions. The same applies to philanthropic individuals and multinational oil companies operating in our various local communities who desire a conducive and peaceful environment to operate in the polity but fail to support most initiatives that will generate such peace. This is partly responsible for the slow development in the youth industry, and the capacity to drive the desired change is weak because not only are the existing structures weak, but those who should ordinarily crave it are themselves marginalized, not empowered, and schemed out. Therefore, empowering the youth sector as its own institution should be the right place to begin national development and rebranding of our nation, because once the youths are left uncatered to, the resultant effect is total failure of the system and youth unrest as we see today. Besides, there is no denying the fact that the burden of transformation and sustaining the entity called Nigeria lies on their shoulders, and if the government continues to turn deaf ears to their yearnings, we only invite more anarchy in the form of digital revolution, as recently witnessed in the Arab world and in other African countries such as Tunisia and Egypt.

This book, therefore, is not like other books on the shelves left there to decorate your library; rather, it's a call to service for many who have not yet identified how they can channel their resources into building a strong community and nation. And this is my personal commitment and contribution to the youths and national development.

In this vein, I therefore recommend this book to all lovers of knowledge and all youths out there, to challenge themselves to contribute to national development through voluntary service. I also recommend that those who manage one NGOs, or voluntary youth clubs, read this book and apply its strategies. The youths will be better for it; I assure you.

Welcome to my changed world and arm yourself with *Practical Perspectives on Youth.* As Napoleon Hill once said, "The ladder of success is never crowded at the top," so join in volunteering for change. May you remain blessed with wisdom as you read and apply its time-tested principles.

Matthew Odianose Dominic, ANIMN

Chapter 1

Who Is a Youth?

Man, know thyself.

—Socrates

This is a commonly asked question in our everyday life, especially during interactions with young persons. In fact, if you ask a forty-five-year-old man this same question, you are likely to hear him say, "I'm a youth even at forty-five." This is because youth has been equated with energy and vibrant life regardless of the age bracket. Some may tell you, "I'm a youth at heart," even when they are well over the age of fifty. Of course, you may begin to wonder what a young person about to clock twenty-one will say if his father of fifty years still claims to be a youth. This brings us to that very crucial issue: Who actually is a youth? The concept of youth has been misconstrued to mean many things with no clear definition or ideology; hence, it is subjected to various interpretations.

The Chambers Dictionary defines youth "as the early part of life of a person."[1] Some psychologists have attempted to

---

[1]   www.chambers.co.uk.

define the word "youth" from different perspectives, while some people from a lay point of view just see youths as leaders of tomorrow. Still others cling to the belief that any person who is young at heart, irrespective of age, automatically qualifies as a youth. Psychologists like G. Stanley Hall defined it as "naturally a period of psychological storm and stress."[2] Others like Margaret Mead have defined youthful age as "the period of an orderly developing of a set of slowly maturing interests and activities."[3]

But some like Anna Freud and others have described youth from the perspective of their deviant nature, defining youth as "naturally and universally a period of rebellion."[4] Jones and Wallace (1992) describe young people as "an index of social ills."[5]

The United Nations (UN) has described youth as anybody between sixteen and thirty-five years of age.[6] The Nigerian National Youth Policy (2001) described youth as "any young person within the age of eighteen to thirty-five years and who is a citizen of the Federal Republic of Nigeria."[7]

Although no acceptable definition has been adopted yet, I have chosen to define youth as any young person, whether

---

[2]   Mike O'Donnell. *Introduction to Sociology*. (London: Thomas Nelson & Sons Ltd., 1997), 447.

[3]   Ibid.

[4]   Ibid.

[5]   Gills, Jones, and Wallace. *Youth, Family, and Citizenship*. (Buckingham: Open University Press, 1992).

[6]   The United Nations defines youths as people between the ages of 15 and 24 but recognises that each region may have its own specific definition of youth. (www.social.un.org/youthyear/docs/UNPY).

[7]   National Youth Policy of the Federal Republic of Nigeria (2001), 3.

physically challenged or not, who is between eighteen and thirty-five years old, on whose shoulders rests the burden of transformation and reengineering of the society.[8]

This is so because every nation looks to its youth segment as future leaders, so the task of building the country lies on them rather than on those outside the youth bracket. That explains why any responsible and responsive government invests heavily in the human resources development of its youth population. Youths are popularly believed to be the leaders of tomorrow, but it is also true that they are the leaders of today because their leadership preparation starts with the values they adopt today for the challenges of tomorrow. They can only assume those responsibilities after they are given the chance to express and implement all they have acquired in form of knowledge and skill.

There is no doubt that youths have a place and role that cannot be taken away from them. Aside from that, they have an identity no matter their status—e.g., disabled or able, married or single, male or female, skilled or unskilled, educated or uneducated, etc.

Youths are agents of social change, as Steven Mills rightly put it when he said, "Young people are barometers of social change, but they do not simply reflect such change; they actively and consciously partake in it."[9]

In the traditional African society and even in the Victorian age in Great Britain, youths and women were only seen and not heard, but with advances in civilisation and education, those barriers are being broken in many traditional and

---

[8]   Matthew O. Dominic, 2001.

[9]   Steven Mills. *Youth Lifestyles in a Changing World* (Buckingham: Open University Press, 2000), 14.

conservative societies across the world. Youths are being given their place of prominence in the scheme of things. The youths still maintain a pride of place in any given society, but if this is traded off, the sad consequences manifest in youth vices and unrest to the extent that everyone loses the chance to sleep with both eyes shut. This is why youths must be allowed to maintain their identity by accepting that they have a say in any matters relevant to their development. Policies that directly or indirectly affect youths should not be put in place without due consultation with these young people, because they are the ones who will eventually, for better or for worse, bear the consequences of such policy,.

Essentially, youths share common features: being young and active in their prime as well as hyperactive sometimes, but unable to switch roles with adults, taking risks no matter how dangerous, including being adventurous with their sexuality. All these attributes make them the most vulnerable among all the different segments of the population. This is corroborated by Steven Mills: "Young people experience a common status in the sense that they are not yet adults and they are often not treated as adults by the adults."[10]

And that is why youth statistics in any census attract meticulous attention: because they usually provide insight into a number of things concerning the dynamics of youth. For instance, it is in such statistics that one will able to locate the number of youths leaving their teenage years, growing to be adults, in the labour force, and at various stages of education. This vital information immensely assists those responsible for initiating youth development policies.

---

[10] Ibid.

Most of us pass through the youth stage, recounting positive or negative experiences. It is one peculiar stage we all wish to relive when we grow old, particularly if we had a blissful experience growing up. It is a period we cannot live through twice, no matter how much we wish it to happen, and that is why young people should be given the right guidance to pass through that stage with minimal interference from parents. The unfortunate twist is that many parents or guardians are afraid to allow their children or wards to make mistakes at this period, so they create a stereotypical pattern of life for them before they even enter their teenage years. When they become teenagers, they are quickly enlisted to live out the script. Although I know some parents do it unconsciously because of their life experiences, they tend to shield the child from experiencing life like any normal teenager and force them to make decisions that may eventually hurt their future without minding the opinion of the teenager at the centre of the crisis. Parents may want the best for their teenagers, but they should always be guided by the fact that they need not make up in their children what they had lost during their own youthful years. Instead, they should allow young people to make their own mistakes under their guidance and learn from them. By so doing we are giving teenagers the independence to think and take more responsibility for their future actions under minimal parental control. I sincerely believe this is the best way for young people to live their youthful lives and retain their youthful identities.

Therefore, the notion of identity is pivotal in the understanding of young people.

Chapter 2

Mobilization of Youths: Five Strategies

There are no limitations to the mind except those we acknowledge

—Napoleon Hill

In times past little effort was put into mobilization of youths for community effort programmes and voluntary services, despite the fact that some voluntary organisations—such as the Boys' Brigade, Boy Scouts, and Red Cross, among others—have existed in other parts of the world for nearly a century.

In traditional African society, the head of the age group is responsible for calling out the youths of the community whenever there are some voluntary services to be rendered. The message is normally passed through the town crier, who announces the meeting for all the youths, requiring them to gather either at the village square or at the home of the clan's head. At either of these designated places of assembly, the job to be done is shared and executed by the young people. This communal effort is done continuously not for any individual's material benefit, but for the benefit of their community.

In recent times, however, there has been a great deal of effort and direction towards youth empowerment, mobilization, and development. This has prompted the creation of many of the voluntary organisations we now have, each helping to increase the desire for community service and re-orientate the youth towards national development. And in recent times, non governmental organisations with interest in different aspects of youth development have sprung up beside the uniformed voluntary organisations that have existed for a long time.

While some have directed their objectives towards sports development and the physical well-being of the youths, some exist to promote healthy living by campaigning against HIV/AIDS, while others work towards eradicating teenage vices such as teenage pregnancy, abortion, armed robbery, kidnapping, drug abuse and trafficking, etc.

The youths remain the most vulnerable sector of any nation, and because they are mostly marginalised or neglected in the scheme of events, they are generally prone to social vices. And because of their vulnerability to social vices of all kinds, there arises an expedient need to effectively mobilise them not just for the benefit of the society at large but also for their own primary benefit.

2.1. Definition of Concepts

In order for us to better appreciate this discourse, I shall provide some definitions of terms being used in this chapter. This shall streamline our areas of concentration to youth mobilization and strategies.

2.11. Mobilization

The Chambers Dictionary defines mobilization "as the way of preparing a group for use or an action."[11] In other words, mobilization of youths can be best described as the act of gathering young people together for a specific goal or to achieve a set objective.

2.12. Strategy

Strategy is a word from the military dictionary that connotes the method employed to fight warfare.[12] In business it is seen as a system for achieving profit either through marketing strategy or by beating competition. Put differently, we can say it's a systematic plan of action adopted to achieve a particular goal.

2.2. Historical Perspective of Youth Mobilization

It is essential to take an historical look into the various ways youths have been mobilised in the past, both for communal and national development, directly from pre-colonial days in Nigeria.

In the old days, youths were often called together by the town crier through the use of a metal or wood gong to participate in community sanitation exercises. Anyone who

---

[11] The Chambers Online Dictionary defines mobilization as the act of mobilizing or preparing something for use or action, etc. (www.chambers.co.uk).

[12] TheFreeDictionary.com defines strategy as the art or science of the planning and conduct of war; generalship (www.thefreedictionary.com/strategy).

failed to participate was fined heavily. This is still practised today in some communities.

In the evenings youths also gathered together to listen to tales by moonlight. It was on such occasions that ancestral stories and their origins were told and certain traditions were passed from one generation to another. However, this invaluable oral tradition is fast disappearing from many communities today. Factors such as modern civilisation and infiltration of western culture have attributed to the erosion of our traditional value system and norms.

Again, in the pre-colonial days youths gathered at the village square on certain days to watch wrestling duels, which were organised occasionally in the community, at times as a rite of passage when boys graduated into adulthood. The emerging adults showcased their strength to the admiration of spectators who, in most cases, were comprised of mostly youths. Thus, traditional wrestling matches provided a good avenue for youth mobilization.

In the colonial and post-independence days of Nigeria, however, the youths were mobilised through political rallies and emancipation movements led by the political gladiators of the time; such as the late Nnamdi Azikiwe, popularly called the Zik of Africa; late Chief Obafemi Awolowo; Herbert Macaulay; et al. They formed political forums and platforms, both abroad and on the home front, where young minds were brought together to discuss national issues, such as the struggle for independence and total eradication of colonialism. One of these platforms was the Nigeria Youth Movement, which later metamorphosed into a political party. It is noteworthy to state that the nationalists were in their prime and at a youthful age when they started the calls for independence.

In fact, many of them went ahead to form various political platforms such as the Nigerian National Democratic Party (NNDP), Action Group (AG), National Council of Nigerian Citizens (NCNC), etc. Their agitation and ability to mobilise youths both at home and abroad no doubt led to the attainment of independence from our colonial masters Britain in 1960.

2.3. National Youth Service Corps

The National Youth Service Corps was established in 1973 by the military government of General Yakubu Gowon. This was another avenue where youths were mobilised for community and national service, and it still exists today.

During their service year, Youth Corps members are deployed to different communities to use their skill to serve the needs of the communities where they are assigned to work. Some are deployed to work in schools or government institutions, while others may be deployed to primary health care centres and even to private establishments. As a result, many Youth Corps members have been able to deploy their knowledge and skills where they are needed through the use of various initiatives, developing self-help projects that contribute to their own quota of development to the various communities across the nation. Of course, some of them received commendation awards for their various contributions, especially those who have been outstanding in their service year.

In addition, the War Against Indiscipline (WAI) was introduced by the regime of General Muhammadu Buhari and the Mass Mobilization for Self-Reliance, Social Justice, and Economic Recovery (MAMSER), which made waves with Professor Jerry Gana as the chief promoter, was made a veritable platform for youth mobilization. WAI was later renamed the War Against Indiscipline and Corruption (WAIC) by the late General Sani Abacha to mobilise youths for national reawakening, value reorientation, and national development through various forms of rallies and programmes designed to sensitise the youths and the entire citizenry. These were some of the ways youths were mobilised for voluntary service to the state. Whether these structures achieved their objectives remains a debate in many circles. The National Youth Service Corps scheme has attracted a lot of debate in recent times. Nigerians continue to question its relevance in the scheme of events, particularly as they are the first object of attack when a conflict arises, as was recently experienced in the Jos Plateau state of Nigeria where the Boko Haram sect descended on innocent young corps members serving in the state.

2.4. Five Strategies of Mobilization

2.41. Formation of Youth Clubs and Volunteer Organizations

One method youth workers can adopt to mobilise youths is to form youth clubs and voluntary organisations in their area of domain by organising regular programmes that will attract these youths to come together for social interaction. Sporting activities, drama and cultural programmes, music talent hunts, dance competitions, fashion shows, etc., are good rallying points for youth mobilization. During enrolment for these programmes, forms should be designed and circulated for the attendees so that they can choose which club they would like to belong to. They should also be made to meet with the leaders of these organisations who, in turn, should be in attendance to receive them. Every programme should be an opportunity to recruit new members into the existing clubs with the benefits clearly stated. For instance, most of the existing uniformed organisations—namely the Boy Scouts, Boys' Brigade, and Red Cross—can be found in almost all the local governments of Lagos State, operating either in churches or schools. All that is required is to approach the head of these clubs to get their programme of events and then work closely with them to oversee their development. Besides that, many of them now have websites where young people can visit, register, and browse through the yearly programme to learn more about the organisation. The non-uniformed voluntary organisations can be located through the various NGOs they are affiliated with or through their respective umbrella organisations and websites, too.

Forming new clubs can be a daunting with little or no financial backing, especially for those working with government institutions; however, the organised private sector have a social responsibility towards these youths who form the bulk of their target market. They can, either through individual or joint initiatives, carry out corporate social responsibility projects that will be beneficial to the community in which they operate and make profits.

In attempting to approach corporate organisations for partnership funding, youth workers or volunteers should approach their programmes from a business angle by stating in the proposal the objectives, benefits to participants, stakeholders, and any other disclosure that may be of importance to the donor.

It is also important to draft a memorandum of understanding (MOU) with the intending sponsor and all stakeholders involved in the project to make them realise what they stand to gain from such sponsorship in terms of audience participation and direct marketing. This MOU should contain the levels of participation expected from the sponsor as well as the limitations and powers to be exercised by all stakeholders in the execution of the programme from start to finish. This will serve as a guide to all parties interested in the success of the programme because they will all share the glory. Unfortunately, most people have been unable to apply this in the development and execution of programmes. That's why it hardly appeals to potential sponsors.

Similarly, those who work for government institutions are being caged with different obnoxious practices that neither encourage partnership with the corporate sector nor promote good practice with young people. For this reason, many youth workers and volunteers find it hard to break that jinx of not being able to execute meaningful programmes for the youths they work with in their communities. Therefore, good practice involves giving adequate training, some appropriate funding, a free hand to organise quality programmes in partnership with whatever organisation shares their vision, and a willingness to invest in whatever project they bring forward. A periodical review should also be put in place to assess the significant result and level of impact of the funded programme, and this should be done by an independent review committee to ensure transparency in judgement and advice appropriately when changes in methodology are necessary. This review can be done quarterly or every six months.

The independent review committee may consist of three nominated executives of the umbrella youth body at the state level, a nominated member from the local executive body, a nominated youth development worker in the zone if there are more than one, a nominated member of an NGO in that zone, the head of the department of youth or nominated senior officer, two nominated young people from the zone, and a legal adviser from the supervising ministry.

These people will not only function as advisers to the supervising ministry of youth development, but act as project advisers to any programme initiated by youth workers in their zone. They will review the progress of any funded project and recommend needed modifications to the supervising ministry.

Another aspect is visiting and regular monitoring events of these newly formed organisations as often as possible to nurture them to maturity and assist them in fashioning quality programmes to keep them busy and productive. As it is for a baby growing up to be supported and nurtured to maturity, so too it is for those new organisations to be supported and find their feet. This also entails the filing of their minutes, attendance, and member statistics, as well as any other report of programmes that will normally form the basis of reporting and future planning.

The independent review committee should also play the role of adviser and partner with them to ensure the successful completion of their yearly programmes.

Good listening and communication skills by professionals are important here, because to be able to work well with young people one should be able to listen attentively and reason from their level of understanding to the level of comfort of the youths.

2.42. Personal Approach

Another way that field officers can mobilise is the personal approach strategy. This strategy is seldom used by field officers because some lack the selling and the public relations skills necessary to promote an idea to a select group of youths. This method has proved to be the best over the years and has stood the test of time. For instance, the founder of the Boys' Brigade, Sir William Alexander Smith, employed the personal approach in recruiting boys into the organisation. He observed the truancy among boys in church at that time and personally approached and convinced them to enrol in his new organisation. Knowing that young boys like music and drums, he introduced band lessons, and this actually attracted young people to the organisation.

In adopting this personal approach, field officers should also take into consideration the interest of their target group and offer them the opportunities or information on where to access them if they cannot provide them immediately. There is no doubt that this approach may sometimes task one's personal resources and time, but experience shows that the result is always worth the effort if it is done with an altruistic mind not seeking personal gratification. Young people should be involved in arranging such placements—or training, as the case may be. It is important to note that the ability to become a resource to youths determines the level of cooperation and patronage one will get. In other words, one should strive to be an encyclopaedia of resources that can connect young people to areas where their needs can be met satisfactorily.

As the Latin saying goes, "*Ex nihilo nihil fit,*" meaning nothing comes out of nothing. Therefore, you cannot offer what you don't have. Aside from regular training provided by employers, one must be updated about current events and information that will benefit the youths. As such, field officers have a responsibility to improve themselves so that they can effectively share knowledge with these youths and attract more young people into whatever group they form with ease. This is how we prove our passion for the work, because once passion is lacking it becomes difficult to be happy doing the job. Adopting this approach will require the field officers to be Web-savvy so that they can direct youths to these opportunities, so that they may take advantage of them. Young people are very good at asking questions during interaction, so those who work with them must be ready with solutions to their puzzles. Good public relations, selling, and communication skills play a significant role in this. Therefore, public relations skills must be sharpened to ensure youth workers can effectively market the new clubs to these young people.

Suffice it to say, we should also be conscious of the fact that many of the youths we work with are more versatile than we think and have so much information in their heads just waiting to explode. In that case, we should be ready to assist them to put their latent ideas into proper practice. This is basically because, in our e-learning age, many youths are influenced by what they see in the media, particularly the electronic media and the Internet—media many youths are seriously addicted to. Unfortunately, these young people are often readily influenced by the wrong things because what they watch is uncensored by their guardians or parents, nor do the authorities strictly censor the media content allowed to be viewed at certain times during the day. This is why outdoor activities should dominate the programmes set for young people rather than allowing them to take solace in the Internet or some other form of addictive behaviour such as gaming or porn, because experience has shown that they are more attracted to such activities, which are becoming the order of the day among our young people. This is also a practical way for parents and schools to engage young people and steer them away from idleness, which makes them vulnerable to vices. Sports programmes such as karate or Taekwondo classes, table tennis or lawn tennis clubs, football, basketball, cycling, swimming, dance and musical groups, and other competitive games should be introduced and encouraged.

Society doesn't always present young people with good role models; hence, youths tend to jump on the bandwagon of bad behaviour. Parents and guardians who want to become good role models must start by getting involved in the activities that interest the young people they mentor, and they must also recognise their limitations, lest they are pushed beyond their ability.

In the same vein, field officers must be conscious of the conflict that arises in care and control and be ready to manage it so that the service users don't lose interest in the activities they are trying to sell to them. Research has shown that the ability to manage the crises that exist in such circumstances determines how much we succeed with the youths. Each time we try to make them see our own point of view and fail to consider their own point of view, it usually results in conflict. Therefore, we should apply a participatory approach so that these youths can make suggestions. We must do this in our planning and decision-making processes, and even if we do not entirely buy their ideas, we must not tell them outright that they are wrong. All you need to do to modify those youthful ideas is suggest practical alternatives that the youths can relate to.

2.43. The Internet

This method is hardly employed due to the low concentration of information technology in Africa. We live in a global village; as such, the world is reduced to a small village where we can reach our audience at the speed of light. Since its inception, the Internet has been a hit among the younger generation and will probably remain so for a long time to come. Therefore, it is not surprising to see their lives lived more in the virtual world than in the real world. What is Internet itself? "The Internet is a network of computers globally connected to one another on a multiple node basis."[13] And the word "Internet" connotes an "international network."[14]

The Internet has become a tool for social mobilization and networking. It is evolving day by day and is so dynamic and sophisticated that there is practically nothing we cannot do on it. We can buy practically anything online—except, for the sake of security, weapons. People meet their wives and girlfriends; do their shopping; do their business without having a physical office, yet make money; and connect with old friends through social networks such Facebook, MySpace, Twitter, and LinkedIn. Again, thanks to the sophistication of mobile devices such as iPhones, Blackberry phones, Androids, and the like, it has become quite easy to connect on the go with most young people who have one or more of these social networks on their mobile phones. Therefore, the Internet cannot be ignored by any forward-thinking individual or organisation wishing to impact the younger generation because we have to meet

---

[13]   G. Omotayo Gbede. *Cyber Marketing*, Lagos, 2002.
[14]   Ibid.

them where they gather. The reality is that only a few organisations in Africa have websites, and those few that do don't have quality content that will attract these youths. The quality of the website content and how the website is promoted determines how far it can sustain visitor interest and the regularity of those visits. The Internet has become a source of networking where different people can connect to one another, no matter where they reside in the world. This shows how much can be accomplished using this new medium of communication to mobilize young people.

There isn't any doubt that the majority of Internet users across the globe access the World Wide Web (WWW), which allows every Internet user to own and customise websites, get information from search engines, read news, watch movies, etc. The majority of people who visit websites are youths, and they do many inexplicable things. Some of the popular sites on the Internet are YouTube, Facebook, Twitter, MySpace, Yahoo, Google, and MSN. The internet remains a meeting place for many service providers and their customers. Organisations and clubs must be encouraged to develop websites with quality content that will attract the large number of youths, because this has proved a very easy and effective way to recruit youths in droves to new organisations in this millennium. Many organisations in the United Kingdom and in the United States already have websites either developed by their members or sponsored by other corporate organisations, with sponsor banners advertised daily on their websites. The Commonwealth Youth Organisation in the United Kingdom website is an example.

Nothing can be gained by stating that the lack of recreational centres in many Nigerian communities has contributed to the youths looking for fun elsewhere, and the Internet has become succour for these young people.

The aspect of funding could be a serious challenge, but sponsorship can make the difference for these organisations. No single organisation can do it on its own, except those that are well funded by their principal or promoters, but with the help of sponsor organisations or donor agencies they can develop their own websites. By doing so, they stand to benefit so much in terms of patronage from this target market.

Organisations that register with the United Nations Online Volunteer programme will find volunteers ready to help them develop a free website, which they can eventually manage with time.

The Internet has also become a networking resource where local clubs and organisations can network with other organisations internationally. They can partake in annual events and international exchange programmes, and access funds from international donors. Once these websites are created, information relating to the organisation stand can be placed for potential visitors to read with adverts soliciting visitors to join these clubs or voluntary organisations. No doubt, the response will be overwhelming. In fact, the websites can attract commercial adverts from blue chip companies, especially online companies (e.g., Google and others) seeking avenues to reach their potential customers. This surely will be another source of revenue to maintain the website and keep it going for a very long time. Therefore, the Internet remains one of the most neglected strategies for mobilization in this present age, and all resources to deploy it should be laid at the disposal of organisations through governmental support and the organised private sector.

2.44. The Media

Utilizing either print or electronic media is another strategy that can be employed in the mobilization of youths. This is because the media, especially with the proliferation of electronic media in and so many media organisations in the country now, gives ample opportunity to those working with youths to access and take advantage of free airspace available for youth content programmes. In Europe, for instance, many children's programmes are aired on television with direct sponsorship from government, so the children can have programmes relevant to their age to entertain them instead of adult programmes they will not benefit from watching. This, however, has not taken full root yet in Nigeria.

However, the various electronic media can create free air programmes with good youth content ready to air to viewers. These could be educational, entertaining, or phone-in programmes on topical issues that affect the youths. This has been a relatively untapped route to get to the youths because statistics have shown that majority of youths are glued to the television more than 60 percent of their viewing time. This is why field officers must develop youth programmes with youth content sellable to the media houses. Through this avenue, field officers can also mobilise youths into various clubs and organisations. There must be consistency in the execution of the programme because any company wishing to identify with it by way of advertising or partnership funding will, among other things, always consider the consistency and the audience reach.

2.45. Direct Membership

Direct participation by membership in these organisations is another proven strategy that has worked for many. This can be achieved by joining those organisations as members, sharing responsibilities and ideas, and participating in all their programmes. While a young boy growing up during my secondary school days in 1985, I had to join a uniformed organisation, the Boys' Brigade of Nigeria, where I rose from the rank of company boy to become an officer. Even after I had finished my university education, I still held my membership as an officer and later became the secretary of the Ikeja Battalion Council until 2003, when I had to pull out to begin my postgraduate studies. In those days I, like other young people, was attracted by the musical instruments we saw young people like us playing. The marching and the uniforms also compelled us to join. The organisation not only gave us the opportunity to acquire musical skills—including how to beat drums and play instruments such as the trumpet, tambourine, bugle, and a host of others—but also made it possible for us to travel to many places for camping exercises and exchange programmes. We also visited places of interest in neighbouring states for days in very harsh conditions. We enjoyed it all the same, though, because those trainings made us more resilient whenever we found ourselves being deprived of anything. In fact, the organisation has turned out lots of young artists and musicians I know today, who all learnt how to play one instrument or the other when they were members. The story may not be the same today, as the Internet and computer games seem to top the chart of things attracting youth attention.

Be that as it may, it doesn't mean we can no longer rejuvenate programmes that will rekindle the interest of our youths. We can now add some things such as computer games to the curriculum to attract young people and sustain their interest. Joining these organisations gives members a deeper insight into how these youth clubs and voluntary organisations function. Some of those experiences can help those who work with young people to harness and channel their energies positively.

Being a member also allows one to share identity with the youths. It makes them want to trust you, as they feel that you understand where they are coming from and you are able to better relate with them on every level. Moreover, being a member confers on you special privileges that others may not have access to, like being their mouthpiece in times of negotiation and advocacy.

Chapter 3

Networking as a Tool for Success

If a loafer is not a nuisance to you, it's a sign that you are somewhat of a loafer yourself.

—John L. Mason

Networking is a tool seldom employed and ignored by many. It has a great deal to offer when its principles are applied correctly and consistently. Networking has been defined by many scholars in different ways.

The Collins Internet Dictionary defines networking as forming business connections and contacts through informal social meetings.[15]

Patricia Dorch views it as "a means of socialisation, meeting people, and sharing information about one another."

There is no doubt that we cannot live in isolation; as the popular maxim states, a tree cannot make a forest. The use of networking to share information and transfer data from one end to another indicates how networking can change things for the better. I have adopted this strategy many times and recorded huge success. For instance, we

---

[15] www.collinsdictionary.com/dictionary/english/networking.

once organised a seminar in London and wondered how we would manage with the invitations given the fact that we were new residents in the area. Fortunately for us, we had registered on a social network popular with many Nigerians in Diaspora known as Facebook. All we did was send random invitations to all our network friends on Facebook, and the response was overwhelming. In fact, I never realised the number of Nigerians hooked up to that network until I used it.

Many opportunities abound when you network; they are unlimited. Some people, however, often think that they don't have the time and resources because networking can be time-consuming. Sometimes you will be required to attend some events and commit some of your resources towards achieving common goals. What some have failed to realise, according to Patricia Dorch, is "that every chance one has to meet new people is an opportunity to network, whether in the office with colleagues or associates or with friends and acquaintances, or at a business luncheon."[16]

It is true that "networking for success takes time," and that's why it has been referred to as a process by Julie Chance, because "Profitability can only be achieved when the process is followed especially if one is networking for business purpose."[17]

According to Nick Corcodilos, "The quality of networking is not judged by the number of contacts you make but the quality of relationships you enjoy."[18]

---

[16] www.selfgrowth.com/articles/Dorch1.html.
[17] http://ezinearticles.com/?expert=Julie_Chance.
[18] www.pbs.org.

When computers are linked together on the same server, they are able to share information and data despite the physical distance between them. Networking works the same way. Each multitasks to achieve a common objective.

Networking in social relationships can be likened to computer networking, and that is why it has been referred to as leverage one can use to attain certain heights in one's life cycle, as suggested by John Mason, who once said, "You cannot rise as high in life as those people who are closest to you."[19]

This assertion is also captured by Joyce S. Osland and others in their writing on power and influence. They posit that people who take the time to cultivate good relationships within the organisation usually receive better service and cooperation from others.

This is a typical phenomenon seen in African, Latin American, and Asian cultures alike; a lot is achieved through personal relationships or networking. This in ordinary parlance is called in Nigeria "Man no man." As a matter of fact, one hardly gets anything in Africa, even what one is legally entitled to, without knowing somebody. This sums up why networking is so essential for youth workers and volunteers in accessing corporate funding for programmes.

I remember how networking helped me achieve success with two important programmes I had organised. The first instance was in 2002, when I was working on a partnership funding agenda for a seminar on youth empowerment and was assigned to work with youth executives in the Somolu local government area of Lagos State. The second occasion

---

[19]   http://ezinearticles.com/?expert=John_L._Mason.

was a workshop on a HIV/AIDS awareness campaign, when some youth leaders and I organised for some youth groups in St. Francis Catholic Church, Oregun-Ikeja, Lagos, in 2003. We had to approach some corporate companies and some well-meaning individuals. Fortunately for us, among those who eventually responded were those we had formal and informal contact with—i.e. top management officers—a direct result of my personal networking over the years.

Networking in social relationship as described by Karen Zastudil is an "ongoing process that can last for a lifetime as a result it becomes a way of life."[20]

In Patricia Dorch's opinion, networking requires mission, goals, vision, and a willingness to share valuable information with others. She further believes that "networking events, meetings, and conferences are places to make plans, reconnect, and stay in touch because it involves building relationships, helping others, and giving advice to anyone who asks." She goes on to state that the objective of networking should not be who you know but who knows you.[21]

Although many scholars have advanced different strategies for successful networking, maintaining that it is a two-way network, mutual concerns must be put into consideration when networking. But I'm more impressed by the strategies advocated by Patricia Dorch and Biba Pedron. Patricia Dorch clearly recommended in her contribution to "Networking: 17 Essential Strategies of

---

[20] http://ezinearticles.com/?expert=Karen_Zastudil.
[21] www.selfgrowth.com/articles/Dorch1.html.

Networking in the 21st Century."[22] She recommended these strategies:

1. Create a good first impression.
2. Exchange business cards.
3. Build a relationship knowing how to hold an effective conversation.
4. Engage your company.
5. Be an active listener.
6. Build trust.
7. Follow up with your network.

Biba F. Pedron, in her article "How to Maximize the Benefits of a Networking Event?"[23] outlined a more comprehensive approach on how to effectively network:

1. Be prepared when you attend a networking event by knowing your goals.
2. Bring your business cards and a pen to take notes on the reverse side of your cards.
3. Practice an effective fifteen-to-thirty-second elevator pitch to sell your service or product.
4. Have a brochure or website.
5. Always be curious and ask questions of others while listening to their answers.
6. Be a problem solver.
7. Go to the event with a partner or colleague and introduce that person to your network.

---

[22] Ibid.
[23] www.selfgrowth.com/articles/Pedron5.html.

8. Send a thank-you note or e-mail to your new contacts.
9. Schedule follow-up meetings with the people you had a good connection with.

3.1. Features of Networking

Networking has its own features. Here are some of its characteristics:

- Networking is a chain.
- Networking has its life cycle.
- Networking has no boundaries.
- Networking shares a common objective.
- Networking shares resources and information.

3.2. Benefits of Networking

1. Networking brings personal success.

Networking has proven to be a serious tool for personal success, and that is why those who network meet people who link them up to other contacts, sharing new ideas on how they can find solutions to pressing challenges. For instance, when I was searching for volunteer opportunities abroad during one of the conferences I attended, I came to know about the United Nations Volunteer scheme, how to register, and how to take advantage of opportunities that come my way. Again, it was through those networking events that I began to send abstracts to conferences, where some were accepted for presentation.

2. Networking is an alternative to an everyday business interaction.

Interacting daily with those you know may not bring the necessary breakthrough you desire, but when you network out of your region and share ideas across the board, you may be surprised to run into somebody who needs what you have and vice-versa. It's like a man finding his lost rib. You are also able to sharpen a project idea because some of your network contacts may have experience in that field or know somebody who does. Networking this way increases your network reach to such an extent that you build a large circle of influence that cuts across borders and race.

3. Networking cuts across all boundaries.

Networking takes you to another level of influence because, in your new network, you will find professionals of different fields who are able to make things happen for you within a short time of connecting with them.

4. Networking is not limited to race or culture.

Networking breaks barriers that may have hitherto existed between cultures and helps us appreciate our differences more without any artificial boundaries. Just like a free-trade zone, or free movement among countries like the Economic Community of West African States (ECOWAS), networking gives you leverage to move among continental and racial boundaries.

5. Networking can serve as a resource centre and advisory centre.

When you network you realise you have a pool of resource professionals to fall back on or connect with when you are planning on executing a project. These people can serve as advisers to the successful hosting of the project.

6. Networking can help bring you into the limelight.
Networking can improve your résumé and give you instant referrals to use when in need of reference. It can also bring you to the spotlight because, if you are a master in your field, people will recommend you to others without your knowledge. There is no recommendation greater than a word-of-mouth one from a satisfied person whom you have networked with in the past.

7. Networking helps to form strategic alliances and acts as a support team.
Networking brings strategic alliances with certain networks, and when these networks are looking for somebody to occupy a particular position, your name is mentioned because they now know your worth and that you can do the job better. The alliance can open new doors of opportunity you may not otherwise get on your own from your circle of friends. During depressing times, you begin to find friends in your network who can serve as a support team and help you go through such difficult times with ease. They may even be closer to you than your family or friends at times because of their professional leanings and are able to provide the necessary support and information you require at that material time.

3.3. Challenges of Networking

1. Cultural and racial differences
Every member of a network must be conscious of the cultural differences that still exist when networking, so do not offend

the sensibilities of others, especially in areas where there may be differences of opinion. Racially opinionated people will sometimes get offended when interacting in common groups if you are not of their race. This is why we should not fail to listen. Allow others to hold their cultural opinions. Although we may be swimming in troubled waters, if we don't listen to others, we will fail in our desire to achieve common goals in the network. To avoid this type of conflict, we must show a high level of sensitivity and avoid discussing topics that can be controversial during a networking event.

2. Overly ambitious network members

When networking, it is common to see some members with overly ambitious ideas trying to bulldoze their way through, which normally results in conflict. Some even adopt unorthodox strategies to get what they want in the network without minding whom they hurt in the process.

3. The tendency to use superiority to bring others down or reduce their self-esteem

During networking, it is possible to find those who will use either their status or race to intimidate others, with the objective of making a statement that they are superior, even in their opinions. They tend to bring others down and make them insignificant in the network. These members can break your confidence, but it is important not to allow ourselves to be intimated by such attitudes when they arise.

4. Distrust among members of the network

In any network there is a tendency for distrust to exist. Some members may have a biased opinion about others or be prejudiced towards certain races due to cultural differences and beliefs. Because of those biases, it will be difficult for them to trust and recommend you, even when they know you can function in the role effectively. To prevent being caught in such a web, it is important to act above board every time and put the network's interests above your own.

5. Loss of confidentiality
Many times when we belong to a network, our profile is freely available to others in it. This information can also be passed on to third parties in the course of interaction. This suggests that there may not always be the confidentiality of information you desire. Don't be surprised to see calls coming from different and faraway places, with people making enquiries about you, your character, or your service availability.

Chapter 4

Civic Duty, Responsibility, and Youths

You cannot carve rotten wood.

—Confucius

A modern and civilised nation recognises the significant role youths play in nation building. As a result, every nation writes a constitution that is cognizant of the civic rights and responsibilities of every citizen. Those rights are usually guaranteed in the constitution. These rights are referred to as inalienable rights by social theorists like John Locke and Thomas Hobbes, and they must be protected by law.

In Nigeria, for instance, the civic rights of every individual youth is guaranteed in the 1999 Constitution of the Federal Republic of Nigeria, and these rights are clearly stated in the National Youth Policy, too, which is also in conformity[24] with the United Nations Universal Declaration of Human Rights and the African Charter on Human and Peoples' Rights, on which Nigeria happens to be a signatory.

Here are some definitions:

---

[24]   ChambersDictionary.com, s.v. "civic," www.chambers.co.uk.

1. *Civic duty* can be described as those duties or obligations for individuals or a group of individuals in a country that they are expected to offer to their own country. Put differently, it is the corresponding set of objectives that correlates with the rights of each citizen.
2. *Civic* means "of, relating to, or belonging to a city, a citizen or municipal or civil society."[23]
3. *Citizen* has been defined as "a person owing loyalty either by natural birth or naturalisation to the protection of a state or a union"[25] The Nigerian constitution describes a citizen as a legal member of the Nigerian state who has full powers to exercise political rights in the Nigerian society to which he or she belongs. Citizenship can be acquired by birth, registration, or naturalisation.
4. *Responsibility*, as defined in the *Chambers Dictionary*, is something that a person has to do, an obligation to be carried out.[26]

4.1. Historical Perspective

Civic responsibility has existed since the time of the Roman Empire, though it became more pronounced with the ratification of the United States Constitution in 1787.

But in Africa, civic responsibility became more popular with the struggle for independence in the late twentieth

---

[25] Ben Ewemie. *Essentials of Citizenship Education in Nigeria* (Benin City: Joeseg Associates, 2000).
[26] Chambers Dictionary.com, s.v. "responsibility," www. chambers.co.uk/search.php?query=Responsibility&title=21st.

century, when people came together voluntarily to fight for the emancipation of their own people from the shackles of oppression and colonialism

The Nigerian youths have always been at the forefront of volunteering their services to the development of the nation and promoting an egalitarian society built on social justice, fairness, and equality.

The first attempt at this happened when some articulate young Nigerians came together in the pre-independence era to form the Nigerian Youth Movement, which later metamorphosed into a political party. Involved in the political activities that engulfed the country in 1960, this movement became a strong force to be reckoned with. This is largely due to the fact that the late founding fathers of our democracy, such as Herbert Macaulay, Dr. Nnamdi Azikiwe, Chief Obafemi Awolowo, Chief Anthony Enahoro, Sir Ahmadu Bello, and a host of others who formed various movements, were all young and in their prime. After their studies abroad, they began the struggle for independence, which later brought about the formation of parties that gradually helped put a stop to colonial rule in Nigeria. Even after independence, their agitation against the Anglo-Nigerian Defence Pact made the Nigerian government abandon the pact because it would have perpetually tied us to the apron strings of the colonial masters. That was when we later became a republic in 1963.

Furthermore, the National Youth Service Corps (NYSC) was established by the military regime of General Yakubu Gowon in 1973 to promote national unity and integration and expose graduates of tertiary institutions to leadership roles and community development projects before joining the labour market. It became another avenue where youths continue to volunteer their services and perform their civic responsibilities to the state today, even under severe threat from enemies of the state.

The National Youth Service scheme deploys those who are under thirty years of age and have completed their university education, whether in Nigeria or anywhere else in the world, on a one-year mandatory service to their fatherland. They are deployed after an orientation exercise in all states of the federation to different villages and towns where their services are needed. They are often posted at hospitals, primary health clinics, local government offices, ministries, government parastatals, and the corporate sector during their primary assignments. The federal government pays them and their employers a monthly stipend. In some cases, they are assisted with accommodations beyond their primary allowances. During their service year, they are expected to individually or collectively identify areas of interest for which they can carry out a project that will be beneficial to the community they serve. No doubt, many Youth Corps members have successfully carried out and launched projects that made positive impacts in their various host communities. For their efforts, many of the outstanding Youth Corps members have been rewarded with national and state awards, which in some cases include automatic employment after their service year.

Another way youths have continually carried out their own civic responsibility is through voluntary youth clubs and organisations such as the Boys' Brigade, Boy Scouts, Red Cross, Ahmadiyya Youth Organisation, Catholic Youth Organisation, Royal Rangers, Girl Guides, Federation of Boys and Girls Clubs, and other nongovernmental organisations. They have continued to serve both humanity and their country through the various programmes and yearly projects they voluntarily carry out in their communities.

Others have volunteered in many other ways through participating as volunteers in organised FIFA-grade football competitions such as Nigeria '99, the 2000 African Cup of Nations, and COJA All African Games 2003 to contribute their own quota to the successful hosting of those games.

4.2. Obligation of Youths to the State

As I mentioned earlier, the youths have rights like every other Nigerian, as enshrined in the Nigerian Constitution, and such rights carry a corresponding obligation on the part of every citizen. The rights, responsibilities, and obligations of the Nigerian youth are contextualised in the provision of Chapter Four of the 1999 Constitution of the Federal Republic of Nigeria, which itemises the fundamental human rights of Nigerian citizens as well as in the Universal Declaration of Human Rights and the African Charter on Human and Peoples' Rights. What this means invariably is that our rights are limited to the extent of our obligation. Therefore, youths are expected as a matter of fact to fulfil all their obligations to the state and ensure that others are encouraged to do likewise. Among such civic obligations of every Nigerian youth as spelt out in the Federal Government National Youth Policy 2001 are the following:

1. Promotion and defence of democracy and civility in the governance of the country and interpersonal relationship with fellow citizens
2. Eschewing ethnic and religious bigotry

3. Eschewing all acts of violence and crimes such as cultism, armed robbery, street violence, alcoholism, prostitution, etc.
4. Active participation in the promotion of national unity, national reconciliation, peaceful coexistence, and good neighbourliness
5. Promotion of self-help, self-respectability, cooperation, and community development
6. Promotion of values of tolerance and responsible conduct
7. Conservation and promotion of the environment against pollution and degradation
8. Respect for and promotion of all symbols of national unity such as the flags, the national pledge, and the national anthem
9. Promotion of a healthy, responsible, and respectable lifestyle free from communicable diseases, alcohol, and drugs
10. Active involvement in the promotion of national unity and national development
11. Strive to be law-abiding, responsible, and enlightened citizens knowledgeable about their right as well as duties and obligations
12. Be good ambassadors of Nigeria abroad and promote international peace and harmony.

4.3. Inalienable Rights of the Youths

The inalienable rights of the youths, as guaranteed in the 1999 Constitution of the Federal Republic of Nigeria, are as follows:

1. The right to life
2. The right to freedom of association or assembly
3. The right to freedom of worship and religion
4. The right to proper education and training
5. The right to family life
6. The right to equal opportunities in employment and access to social services
7. The right to be provided with the special treatment in case of disability that his or her condition requires
8. The right to opinion and expression
9. The right to security of life and property
10. The right to leisure, cultural, and sporting activities
11. The right to adequate shelter, health care, social and food security
12. The right to participate in decision making in matters that affect them
13. The right to good and clean environment
14. The right to privacy, family life, and noninterference in personal matters such as correspondence
15. The right to equal protection under the law
16. The right to be protected against harmful traditional practices
17. The right to participate in national development, including matters that affect them
18 The right to protection against the dangers of substance abuse, alcoholism, sexual harassment and exploitation, HIV/AIDS, secret cults, and gender discrimination
19. The right to survival, social, economic, and cultural development

These rights and obligations are expected to be the key commandments youths must adhere to as a matter of culture but most of the time that only exists in principle and not in practice. The reason is that if they are not routed in our norms, it hardly supports young peoples' characters. In other words, they do not see the rationale behind observing these obligations or rules. This brought me to a model I developed from our cultural attributes, which I had chosen to call the four Rs of relationship namely rights, responsibility, respect and reward.

4.4. Four Rs of Relationships

1. Rights

Rights are those liberties that confer on us our human dignity, and this is why social theorists refer to them as "inalienable." In other words, they can neither be taken away from us nor denied. Youths must know their rights, because nobody gets on a journey without having a map of where he or she is going. With our traditional norms and values, certain rights are always conferred on us by nature that, at any point in time, cannot be denied us. For instance, the first-born male child is always taken to be the heir to the family and, in the absence of the father, is consulted for any major decision. Such a right can never be taken from him unless he decides to trade it off, like Jacob in the Bible. These rights are maps that should guide our conduct. It is difficult for someone to trample on your rights when he knows you are knowledgeable about them. He therefore treads cautiously when dealing with the others, realising that he could be checkmated if he crosses the line and there are sanctions to be handed out.

2. Responsibility

Responsibility is defined as an obligation we are required to carry out either to the state or to one another. In our African culture we are taught how to be responsible to others, whether they are family or not, as long they are under our care. Over the years we have grown to embrace the culture of responsibility towards others or, simply put, to be our brother's keeper. When people conscientiously carry out their responsibility towards one another, society judges these people as responsible. For instance, a father who pays his children's school fees and sees to their educational, physical, and mental development would definitely be judged responsible for those children, while those who do not are judged irresponsible. That, in effect, is how it is between the state and its citizens: A state that makes provisions for the mental and physical development of its youths by providing infrastructural facilities—such as good schools, primary health care clinics, good recreational and sports centres, and welfare benefits for the unemployed, or programmes that would meaningfully engage its skilled or unskilled youths, levelling the playing ground for young people to realise their dreams after completing education or training—is practically viewed as not only a responsible government but a responsive government. Such a state would surely get the cooperation of its youths because they would feel compelled to repay the state's efforts by carrying out their obligations without the force of law, whether by paying taxes or whatever else is required. Young people would consciously do this because it is already given and written in their hearts. Because they stand to benefit, they are unlikely to act otherwise.

3. Respect

Respect is not only synonymous with African culture but a norm practised from one generation to another. Once a child begins to grow, he is taught how to respect both older people and authorities by the way he greets and relates to older citizens. This may not necessarily be the case because some youths can be highly disrespectful and sometimes rebellious in their character. When children spend most of their developmental years with different fathers or no father figures in their lives to teach them common morals, it is very difficult for them to develop values like respect for elders or authorities. When a child is well behaved and shows respect in Africa, such a child is said to have come from a good home. It may not necessarily be a perfect home, but to a large extent the values children are taught normally stick with them as they grow into adults. They, in turn, pass these values to their own children when they become parents. This is why respect is an important virtue that young people must be taught from their adolescent stage until they become adults, further enhancing their relationships not only among themselves but their relationships with others and the state.

4. Reward

Reward is a system of compensation or benefit one gets for fulfilling his or her own side of the deal or bargain. It is also the same with relationships, and that's why when a person who knows and discharges his responsibility, showing respect to others or the state, the rewards that come with it are always monumental and reciprocated. For instance, a child who discharges his duties to his parents and respects them bountifully reaps more love and protection from his parents. In the same manner, a youth who knows his or her rights, discharges the responsibilities to the state, and shows respect to state laws would also be rewarded with care and protection from the state. Therefore, reward is the ultimate benefit of observing and practising the other three Rs of relationships.

4.5. Conclusion

For youths to enjoy those rights already guaranteed by the constitution, it follows that they must eschew all negative behaviour and embrace only positive attitudes that will put them in a position to contribute their own quota to national development. This is so because youths often get misdirected and seek rebellious options in driving home their points when they are denied certain rights or privileges. Therefore, as the popular dictum says, "He who comes to equity should come with clean hands." In the same vein, when youths demand their rights from the state, they must be ready at all times to make sacrifices to carry out those responsibilities or obligations corresponding to their rights. By doing so, they will be justifying any rebellious actions they take against the state or its institutions if their civic rights are denied.

Every right of the youth, however, is limited and not absolute in the real sense; as such, those rights can be denied or revoked. For instance, the right to life can be revoked if a youth is found guilty by a competent court of a capital offence such as murder or armed robbery. In other words, youths must be conscious of the limitations of their rights and act in such a manner that their rights will always be protected by the constitution.

Chapter 5

Youths and Crime

Associate yourself with men of good quality if you esteem your own reputation, for it is better to be alone than in bad company.

—George Washington

Youths are always associated with one crime or another, often because of their vulnerability to negative societal influences. Sometimes youthful exuberance can also lead some of them to participate in crime just for the perverted sense of adventure. This is why when people see a group of youths gather, even for a lawful purpose, they may associate such gathering with trouble. If a crime happens in an area, the first suspects taken in for questioning are usually youths within that area. This kind of stereotyping of youths happens everywhere. That is because people are always quick to stereotype youths as if it is in their nature to commit crime without considering that those committed by adults may be worse. This is why Marxists relate crime to the power structure. "It is people with power who make laws and criminalise those who threaten their interest."[27]

There is no doubt that the high rate of crime in our societies today is engendered by those within the youth bracket. Simply put, youths constitute the highest percentage of those involved in one form of crime or the other. And most often, assumptions are made without any investigation of the social factors responsible for many of these youths getting involved in one crime or the other, when they should be using their productive years engaged in productive activities.

The act of stereotyping, unfortunately, blocks and obscures our sense of judgement and criminalises these youths even more, thereby increasing their vulnerability levels. This is still very prevalent in today's society and even in some advanced countries. For instance, whenever youths gather together to banter with their peers in most neighbourhoods in the United Kingdom, before you can say "Jack Robinson," the elderly citizens living in that neighbourhood have called the police on the presumption that some trouble may ensue in the course of their interactions. As if that's not enough, you see some retail companies installing devices around their shops to dispel youths gathering in their vicinity. This raises several questions about the need for such stereotyping practices against the youths. If you took the time to read the papers and listen to the news coming out of that region from 2008 until 2011, there were many stories of youths brandishing knives all around London, killing one another as if life did not matter to them. In Africa youths are involved in armed robbery, burglary, drug trafficking, Internet fraud,

---

[27] Susan and Peter Calvert. *Sociology Today.* (Hertfordshire: Harvester Wheatsheaf, 1992), 245.

kidnapping, and activating bombs, as recently witnessed in Abuja and some northern states of Nigeria. Between 2008 and 2009 alone, the city of London had experienced too many stabbing deaths, with statistics showing the worst record in the history of the country.

The government was so concerned that it quickly proposed legislation to address the ugly situation, but the measures put in place have not effectively curbed knife crime; instead, many saw it as a cosmetic approach. Although current statistics released by the authorities appear to reflect a drop in knife crime in London, recent killings of young people in 2011 alone have put those statistics in doubt.

Research has revealed that most knife crimes involve youths in their teenage years. Perpetrators go as far as stabbing their victims to death without any respect for the law or sacredness of life. There is little wonder that knife crime constituted the largest youth crime in recent times in some parts of the United Kingdom in 2008.

Consequently, the crimes don't seem to have abated yet, because the government appears to be disconnected from the needs of today's youths. That may account for why the knife has become the devil's hand tool.

In Africa, jobs for skilled or unskilled youths are becoming increasingly difficult to find. There are no sustainable policies to address the welfare of these youths; therefore, they easily resort to crime. The whole drama makes one weep for the kind of society modern-day civilisation has created.

The question to be asked now is this: what factors are generating this crisis among the youths, and why don't they seem to be engaged enough to find productive things to do?

Many scholars have listed different reasons and even proffered solutions, yet there seems not to have been any qualitative result. I am of the view that this gap is usually caused by the systemic failure inherent in the way policies are formulated without the direct participation of the beneficiaries themselves. Most of the time realistic objectives are not set; instead, there are unrealistic objectives and tight time framework that often fail to take into account the dynamism of the actual problem in question. This leads us to ask the pertinent question: what is crime and its causes?

5.1. What Is Crime and Its Causes?

Crime is a very broad subject that cannot be exhaustively discussed within the scope of this book, but the interest here is to take a critical view of how youths get involved in crime from the social perspective and find ways to control it.

Some sociologists have attempted to define crime and equate it with deviance. Although crime has been argued to be similar to deviance, it cannot be entirely equated with it. This is because of its cultural relativity. What may be an acceptable behaviour in one society may not necessarily constitute deviance in another. Homosexuality, for instance, was once commonly considered as a form of deviance in traditional societies, but it is fast becoming a way of life among some young people in Europe, although in Africa it still remains an aberration of a sort. Moralists argue that it is a crime against nature because, for them, it is attempting to reorder nature.

Deviance in its simplistic form is described as the tendency for people to exhibit certain behaviours in a direction that may be against societal norms or not in concordance with the acceptable way of life in a particular society.

According to labelling theorists, represented by sociologists including Edwin Lemert, Howard Becker, and Erving Goffman views crime as the result of social processes in which actions by certain people at certain times come to be labelled as criminal by others."[28]

While the realist believes that crime truly exists, linking it to fear existing in the human mind, the Sociobiologists have linked crime to the biological construct of human beings with societal influences.

Functionalists have advanced theories suggesting that what makes youths behave this way can be ascribed to both historical and social factors, such as age group, peer influence, etc.

In the same vein, some sociologists have opined that it can be ascribed to the differences in individual cultures and societies. Put differently, youth involvement in crime is relative to the kind of environment they live in. Therefore, they are a by-product of their immediate environment.

For the Marxist proponents, however, youth behaviour can be attributed to the class and power system with class factors such as occupation and income playing significant role.

The modernists have propagated that education is the reason, especially because education has now become a universal right and legal requirement for every child. Their belief is premised on the fact that there was less crime in the olden days, when education was mainly enjoyed by children of the upper and royal classes. With that barrier broken now, many youths from different classes have access to cheap education, and that has changed their orientation about

---

[28] Tony Lawson and Tim Heaton. *Crime and Deviance.* (New York: Palgrave Macmillan, 1999), 90.

practically everything, including crime. This is, however, a dangerous position to assume because education is the only tool for liberation and empowerment for the youths and, as such, cannot be denied them. Therefore, a child has the fundamental human right to be educated.

Whether these assumptions and theories are still relevant today or not, however, becomes an intellectual discourse for professionals, social workers, and researchers to disprove.

Needless to say, there are many reasons that huge numbers of youths are involved in crime today. These reasons range from failure of the society itself to government and its institutions, policy formulation failure, the family system, decline of religion in many civilised societies, etc.

Consequently, I would like to submit that crime goes beyond just environmental influences; instead, crime should be seen from a multidimensional approach as a result of the interplay of both societal and dynamic factors in an ever-changing society. This is propelled by the fact that some things that were taken to be crime in the past no longer pass for it now; thus, we must begin to take a different approach to why youths are involved in crime. Aside from that, many children grow up in metropolitan cities where parents have to work several hours with little or no time to care for the emotional and psychological needs of their children, so the burden is on young people to find a parent figure in their lives. When young people also lack mentors and positive role models, they become vulnerable and more likely to resort to crime.

Furthermore, uncensored electronic media and the Internet have exposed the youths to so much violence and crime. As a result, they have become more vulnerable to what they see every day on television screens and the Internet. It is only natural and common sense for them to practice what they see, especially when they have so much latent energy that is not being channelled positively. The youths have been left on their own for so long that their development rests on external forces instead of internal forces like a cohesive family system, which will inculcate strong values in them. How else can a society filled with divorces and broken marriages bring up children who are responsible to the society? This accounts for why the number of youths engaged in teenage pregnancy, drugs, and other forms of social vices keeps rising. The actual crisis is being underestimated everywhere by politicians.

Again, most of the efforts put in by various governments have remained curative instead of preventive, and because prevention has been proven to be better than cure, we must not ignore or downplay the effect of preventive initiatives no matter the cost.

The family remains the bedrock of the society, as posited by Aristotle, and that is why today's governments must do more to engage families in dynamic ways, assisting them to meet their family demands so the young ones have some positive values to fall back on in periods of crisis. Every young person experiences a crisis at one time or the other—some about their identity, some about values, morals, faith, liberties, etc. But if they learn positive values early in life without gaps experienced in their development as a teenager, whether they have one parent or not, that helps them to become more responsible and well-rounded individuals when they grow older.

5.2. Challenges of Combating Youth Crime in Nigeria

Combating and reducing youth crime in Africa have become somewhat Herculean tasks for government and its various agencies. This is partly as a result of the kind of society we have created for our youths. My enforcement in this belief is premised on the glorification of material substance and the elevation of materialism in the society. Youths of today no longer see anything wrong with stealing if the politicians are doing it and being hailed by their kinsmen. Therefore, there is nothing wrong if they steal, too, by Internet fraud. In fact, it is more like a taboo in today's African society for one to be appointed to a political post or a place of honour yet, at the end of the day, fail to amass wealth even for unborn generations.

Similarly, like the sociologists have maintained, I tend to agree that the increase in youth crime today is a direct offshoot of the kind of society we live in, even though this may not be the only reason.

Although today's society is very dynamic and fast-moving, policies in place do not seem able to keep pace with the changes. This is why I strongly believe that for policies to meet their stated objectives, they must be proactive rather than reactive. Unfortunately, most policies in place in Africa— Nigeria, for instance—are often reactive. That's why we need a sharp departure from that cycle to be able to effectively control youth crime.

History has shown that there is no society without youth crime; it only differs in degree. How each country is able to manage its own level of crime depends largely on the strategy deployed and support mechanisms set up in the form of institutional changes reflecting modern realities.

To correct this, many have posited increasing the moral and religious content in our school curriculum right from the elementary stage. While this is welcomed, it is still not certain how far that measure can help because religion itself has been described by Karl Marx as the opium of the people. Aside from that, some fundamentalists have exploited the ignorance of their followers by using religion to plant discord and whip up sentiments against the state, as it has been experienced in many places in the north, including the Boko Haram crisis and others in the past. But suffice to say that there cannot be a sane society without inculcating good morals and respect for values. The fear of the supernatural being "God" is not present in today's youths, particularly when the parent fear factor is always absent. Religion helps to instil the fear of a higher power, and we have seen youths no longer fear the repercussions of breaking the law. Some may disagree with this opinion, but in my practice I have seen young people fear something more supernatural, which they cannot explain, rather than the law they can quote. One can often observe that when a child commits an offence and is told it will be reported to the father or mother (depending on which parent he or she is closest to), the child naturally becomes afraid of what punishment awaits him. But in today's society, parents are becoming less and less involved in the lives of their teenagers, particularly when they are separated from the spouses, and it becomes difficult to instil the necessary discipline and fear factor into them. Little wonder that youths of today grow up not to fear or respect elders, authorities, or others. It is this vacuum that religion fills in the lives of these youths, and such chances should never be blown away on the altar of science or any human philosophy. As the Holy Bible itself puts it, "The fear of God is the beginning of wisdom."[29]

---

[29] *The Good News Bible: Today's English Version*, Proverbs 1:7. (Lagos: St Paul's Publication, 1990.

In addition, religion has proved over the years to be a better alternative to nothing, and if children are properly guided in the way of God no matter the religion, as long it doesn't teach false doctrines and its teaching is in accordance with natural and common laws, young people will always follow it. It stays with them for life. Even if they digress later when they are adults, they already know the difference between good and evil.

Another factor that has challenged the effort of curbing youth crime is that some laws related to punishment are either too harsh or punitive in nature. For instance, in places where punishments for juvenile crimes are supposed to be reformatory, the institutional facilities provided to actualise these sentences are either not existing or scantily available and do not support a corrective process. It surely would produce the opposite result. Sadly, no meaningful progress can be made in this area if the provision—like accommodation for inmates, for example—is too dehumanising and intolerable for the reformatory process to work, and if those looking after their welfare are not well equipped to deal with the inmates.

Similarly, there is a lack of comprehensive rehabilitative programmes that empower inmates after they are discharged that quickly reintegrate them into society. Most of these activities are being carried out by Non-Governmental organisations and religious groups with little or no meaningful funding or appropriate training.

In this vein, government at various levels should support these initiatives by providing such organisations regular partnership funding to complement their meagre funds and enhance the law in this area so that vulnerable rehabilitees are not taken advantage of. The enacting laws to make foundations and organised corporate sectors play an active role in the rehabilitation process have to be instituted after a careful and wide consultation with all stakeholders, just as it was with the amnesty programme with ex-militants in the Niger Delta. There is no doubt that peace cannot be achieved until all stakeholders come together and consider the interest of all, working out a strategy for an enduring peace.

Another setback in reducing youth crime in Africa is the poor dispensation of justice for youths involved in crime. It is disappointing to see teenagers or youths who have exhibited antisocial behaviour being lumped together in the same confinement room with armed robbers, hired assassins, and other hardened criminals. And the delay in dispensing of such cases worsens the problem. The juvenile justice system is in urgent need of reform if our young people go into prison and come out worse off than when they went in.

Again, the high level of unemployment, particularly in our cosmopolitan cities, adds to the challenges faced in curbing youth crime. The non-existence of white-collar jobs and lack of incentives for industrialists to create jobs, coupled with the absence of entrepreneurial initiatives that will employ the growing number of university graduates, have contributed in no small measure to the level of crime we have today.

5.3. Practical Initiatives to Reduce Youth Involvement in Crime

The Role of the Family

The family system was meant to be the first socialisation agent and to serve as a springboard for the mental, social, and physical well-being of the child. Where necessary, it is supposed to act as checkmate so that the child doesn't become a social burden to the family or society at large. Some psychologists have posited that children brought up in a family setting are more likely to develop well mentally, physically, and morally if they are not subject to abuse or neglect. This is because it's most certain that both parents will find time to watch what their children are doing, the kind of company they keep, and what they do outside the home, in school, and other places. When the child misbehaves there are always corrective sanctions like spanking the child's buttocks or withdrawal, even outright denial, of certain benefits enjoyed by that child. However, the issue of punishment has become subjective because of difference in cultural interpretation.

The Holy Bible has enjoined parents not to spare the rod to spoil the child, though this may be interpreted wrongly. The degree of appropriate punishment now remains a debatable issue among scholars and social workers as they seek to set a benchmark commonly acceptable to the society in which they exist. We must not ignore dialogue before discipline when a child misbehaves, and it must be appropriate to the age and maturity of the child.

Aside from that, research has shown that the burden of raising responsible children cannot be left to single parents alone, especially those who live in our ever-busy cosmopolitan cities.

Parents must brace themselves for the fact that there is a time bomb on their hands; the earlier they defuse it, the better for them and the society. We cannot have a sane society where even the family, supposedly the bedrock of the society, is found seriously wanting and in crisis.

Parents should also be involved in getting their children to participate in outdoor activities more than indoor games and being glued to the television. For instance, register them in after-school clubs, sports, drama clubs, and music lessons where they can develop their talents while engaging in other extracurricular activities that may catch their attention at the early stage of their adolescence. Laws that promote family cohesion and reduce pressure on parents need to be constantly promoted so employers can create flexible hours for parents to take out time and be with their children when it matters most. Unfortunately in Africa, this kind of flexibility is lacking in our labour practices, and the earlier we begin to make provisions for it so that parents can take time off work at intervals to be with their children, the better off the society will be.

Parents should increase their control over their children and wards when necessary, especially when it comes to censoring what teenagers watch on television, the hours they are allowed to be on the Internet, and sites they are allowed to visit. This is because research has shown that too much freedom often leads to poor discipline and a poor sense of values among the youths. When youths have the right values instilled in them as they are growing, however, they stay with them for many years to come, and they in turn pass it to other generations.

The Role of Government

The government has the largest responsibility to ensure the sustenance of the family through the laws it enacts. Each government must increase its level of support for the family system by creating policies that will encourage family cohesiveness, reducing the incidence of broken homes, and creating multi-door channels for reconciliation for families undergoing marital challenges.

Consequently governments need to do more in order to curb the incidences of youth crime by getting youths more involved in community service, including it in their academic curricula from the start. By doing so youths would get into organised youth clubs through the various voluntary organisations, organising open days in secondary schools, for instance, where these teenagers can come together, interact with leaders of these organisations, and meet their role models and mentors. They can be enrolled in any one of these organisations this way. And by making it coursework, it now becomes a compulsory course in our primary and secondary schools where marks are given. It is my belief that, by doing this successfully during the year, we would succeed in introducing more youths to the volunteer sector early in life. Many of them may initiate community service projects that will benefit their immediate community. There is no doubt that this will make them tools for social cohesion and control in their immediate community, because I have gathered from my research that no youth involved in community service will want to go out of the way to destroy that same society or allow others to do same. They will go any length to stand for the community and defend it without expecting any reward. This will now give rise to several awards programmes to celebrate those who excel in their community service while still in school—awards such as the Duke of Edinburgh's Award for youths in the United Kingdom and the resuscitation and creation of other youth awards in Nigeria, which have been relegated due to lack of focus in policy direction and funding.

The government should, through its agencies, constantly increase the censoring of media content for children on television. It should also sentence those youths convicted of crime to more community and retributive service than behind bars.

Government also needs to increase funding to the youth sector and enhance the policy in that sector to reflect current trends in meeting the needs and aspirations of the vulnerable sector of the society. This can only be achieved by due consultations and enhancement of the laws in this sector. Besides that, more sport centres and skill acquisition centres should be built to get our youths busy. These centres can, in due course, be passed on to private organisations or nongovernmental organisations who have the right expertise to manage for a certain number of years under an operation, development, and transfer plan instead of government getting directly involved in managing such centres.

The youths, too, should be given more voice in matters that concern them before any law is enacted in that regard. Their voice can be sought through their organised representatives or any forum where their opinions can be aggregated, because when they are involved, the law becomes a part of them rather than them being alienated by those laws.

During the period when military fiat or force was employed in tackling youth unrest, such tactics never achieved any proven, effective solution for youth restiveness, and events have proved such techniques out of date. Therefore, the problem must be viewed from a social angle for such methodology to make any meaningful impact. Even though youth crime cannot be entirely eliminated, different levels of results can be attained over time by consistently putting the right systems in place to discourage it. Achieving a controllable reduction in the number of youths that take solace in crime is a challenge for all stakeholders to work out.

Maintaining adequate records, using information technology in the juvenile justice system, and sharing data among institutions will greatly enhance the quick dispensation of justice and curbing of serial offenders.

The need to review and constantly enhance the laws relating to youth development cannot be overstressed because, aside from the fact that some laws are becoming outdated, not much can be achieved in this area without the legal framework to bring forth the desired result. Those responsible for formulating policies in the national and state assemblies should be conscious of how effective legal framework can enhance youth development and always set in motion such drives that will bring laws in constant touch with realities after proper consultation with stakeholders—i.e., youths or their representatives.

The Role of Religious Bodies

In Africa, particularly in Nigeria where there is a proliferation of religious bodies, one would have expected the level of youth crime to be very low, but unfortunately the reverse is the case.

This is why the religious bodies and organisations must be involved in assisting the government with qualitative programmes that will help to engage the youths. They should also form NGOs that could bring about entrepreneurial initiatives, because what the youths need now is access to training and empowerment, not necessarily hand outs. This cannot be provided by government alone, and for this reason each religious organisation should see it as a point of duty to the society to support and create avenues that will bring empowerment to the greatest number of youths in their communities.

The government and religious organisations can provide infrastructures in their local communities, such as sporting facilities and Internet facilities, that will attract more youths to get busy but strictly monitor their behaviour to ensure those facilities are utilised for their intended use. On the other hand, they can collaborate with other NGOs to identify the basic needs of the youths in their various communities and provide them with the essentials. No doubt this role sharing and partnership will reduce the burden on government, its institutions, and families.

Doing this will also enhance the capacity of religious organisations to sell their own programmes and get tax rebates from government from time to time for investing in the youth sector. The problem with many of these religious bodies is sometimes they either lack the courage to take on the tasks or they possess poor vision. Instead of sitting back waiting for government to call on them, they should be at the forefront of championing causes like this. The early missionaries that brought the Bible to Africa have demonstrated that true religion can actually impart positive values on people if done with the right intentions. The missionary school, for example, remains one of the best schools to send a child to learn, and those who had the opportunity to attend remain living testimonies to this. Essentially, religious bodies cannot sit aloft or take the backbench when society is experiencing serious unrest while they carry on as if nothing is happening. If they do, they, too, will never have true believers. Therefore, the time for them to take back the mantle cannot be overemphasized if history will have anything to record for them.

The Role of the Non-Government Organisation

Various nongovernmental organisations and voluntary organisations are stakeholders in the project of achieving a well-coordinated policy framework in youth development and empowerment. It is basically for this reason that they must continue to evolve programmes on a continual basis to take our youths off the streets and put them into more productive activities. There is no doubt these organisations have a complimentary role to the various levels of government, but they need to take a leading role in directing certain policy initiatives because they work with these youths and thus have a feel of their pulse. They should, therefore, act as youth advocates rather than be allowed to be treated as backbenchers in youth affairs. In some cases, we see an exhibition of those acts that we regularly frown upon the political class committing. For some youth leaders, service in these organisations has become a tool for achieving their personal ends or ambitions, relegating the essence of youth services secondary. Although there is nothing particularly wrong with young people who aspire to lead voluntary organisations being ambitious, when those ambitions conflict with the primary objective of serving constituents, they become an aberration and a disservice to humanity. The lofty objectives of setting up that organisation are defeated on the altar of greed and individual aspirations. Therefore, those who wish to serve others in any capacity must be guided by the utilitarian goal of offering service that will generate the greatest benefit to the greatest number of the young ones they serve. By doing this, the ship is not wrecked midway, and other benefits normally will follow when service is done in its altruistic sense, rather than for what one intends to gain from it individually. Giving other young, promising youths the opportunity to lead and become advocates for their organisations should be a thing of joy and the most honourable act, after one has crossed the youth bracket age, in order not to set the wrong precedent that usually causes friction and encourages dictatorship, monopoly of power, and disenfranchisement of the other youths.

Furthermore, these organisations should be courageous enough to call the government to account when they fail in their responsibility towards the youth sector, because they remain one of the pressure groups that can make a government sit up. If they fail in this task, then they either do not know their rights or have compromised their standing.

Suffice it to say, there is a need to speak with one voice and bury differences when coming together under the umbrella of youth agenda, rather than flying different agenda or allowing politicians with selfish interests to infiltrate their groups and sow discord and division among those who will cater to their own ambitions.

Every responsible government strives to listen to the young ones, just like a father will listen to his child, and as a result those who represent the youths should never be weary in making sure the government hears them, provides for their welfare, and protects their rights.

The Media

The media, being the watchdog of the society, has a pivotal role to play in the reduction of crime in our society. Aside from regularly reporting crime, they have a duty to the society to educate our young people on the dangers crime poses to society as a whole through the various forms of communication, be it electronic or print. Electronic media outfits such as radio or television should consistently air educational programmes that will engage our youths in meaningful thinking and discovery. The media must also look ahead to constantly create publicity and advocacy for those areas in law that require changes, helping our policy makers make good laws to combat youth crime and expose any bad legislation that stagnates youth development in the country.

The relevance of the media in the twenty-first century cannot be undermined, judging by recent events that have happened in other parts of the world. If we are to make any meaningful progress enacting those laws that will develop our youth sector, the media must be 100 percent active in initiating policies, because they have so much information that, if ignored by any forward-thinking government, it could be catastrophic.

In many developed societies, the media shapes the nature of law and almost everything that has to do with developmental initiatives; however, in Africa there seems to be a snail-like approach to addressing important issues. Therefore, the media must be a trailblazer in the direction of policies because they possess the weapon of the pen, which can alter the cycle of history.

Chapter 6

Youths and HIV/AIDS

Men will spend their health getting wealth; then gladly pay all they have earned to get health back.

—Mike Murdock

6.1. Introduction

Since it was discovered in 1981, acquired immunodeficiency syndrome (AIDS) has been the fourth-largest cause of death globally and one of the leading causes of death in Africa.

This disease has, in more than three decades, influenced policies among African governments and attracted world attention. Although no one denies the existence of the disease any longer, the rate at which youths contract the disease makes it very important for AIDS to remain a focal point of policy makers and policy implementers to see what can be done to reduce its spread.

If left unchecked, a disease of this nature is capable of wiping out an entire youth population. It is for this reason that many governments and non-governmental bodies (NGOs) are proactive in the enlightenment of young people in particular against this deadly disease.

Enlightenment of young people is key to stopping the spread of AIDS. Youths are the most vulnerable and active segment of the society, and because poverty is prevalent among many youths, that also increases their chance of contracting the disease.

Secondly, youths are more likely to be in poor health after they are exposed, because they often leave sexually transmitted diseases untreated for long periods of time.

Thirdly, they tend to yield to pressure and exchange money for sex—i.e., prostitution—because they migrate more easily in search of greener pastures, which increase their chances of engaging in risky sex.

Again, in our African society, where sexual gratification has become a practice for getting things like jobs, money, or even certain basic benefits, it puts the female youth on the receiving end with no choice but to cave in to the oppressor.

Furthermore, in Africa, where discussing sex with young people is taboo, they end up taking advice from their peers, who like themselves are inexperienced with sex. The fear of confiding in their parents or being too lazy to read about STDs leaves young people carrying these diseases for too long.

But no responsible nation will sit down and fold its arms, watching its youth force waste away as a result of HIV, which ultimately leads to AIDS.

It is a common fact today that many people live with this disease, and some are still able to live a good life due to the attention the disease has drawn around the world. AIDS is still attracting lot of funding and assistance from international organizations and donor agencies the world over. The enormous effect of the HIV pandemic on the youth population cannot be denied or swept under the carpet. It is partly for this reason, and to save our unborn generation, that many advanced countries like the United States of America, United Kingdom, and other developed countries have teamed up with the United Nations to set up a global fund to fight the disease and provide basic medical care to those already living with the virus, particularly in Africa where the disease is prevalent.

6.2. Brief Statistics about HIV/AIDS

- According to the Family Health International Report (2001), HIV was discovered in 1981 but can be traced back to 1950.
- It is caused by a virus called human immunodeficiency virus.
- No fewer than twenty million people have died of AIDS since it was discovered.
- No fewer than forty million people are presently living with the disease.
- No fewer than twelve million persons are presently living with HIV in Nigeria.
- In Nigeria, the Federal Ministry of Health antenatal clinic's 2008 survey shows the percentage of carriers is about 2.98 million people, the majority of whom are between the ages of fifteen and twenty-nine. The highest death by age bracket recorded is between twenty-five and twenty-nine years.
- The 2009 FMH report showed that about 192,000 deaths have been linked to AIDS.

- It was reported in 2009 that the prevalence of the disease among pregnant women is 4.6 percent, lower than the 5.8 percent reported in 2001. This is clear evidence of a drop in the number of pregnant women contacting the disease.
- By geographical distribution, the survey also showed that the prevalence of HIV/AIDS is lowest in the southwest at 2 percent, while it is highest in the southern region at 7 percent.
- The first known case of HIV in Nigeria was a teenage girl.
- Eighty percent of HIV infections in Nigeria were made possible through sexual intercourse.
- In 1998, statistics revealed that 60 percent of the 20,334 AIDS cases reported in Nigeria were within the age group between 15 and 24 years of age.

(Handbook prepared by GHAIN & Family Health International, 2001

National Agency for Control of AIDS [NACA] progress report, 2010, to the United Nations General Assembly Special Session)

6.3. Why Youths Are Vulnerable

Inadequate Information about Reproductive Health

Young people today prefer to seek information on many more things than just their health. Despite having access to more information about sex than their parents had in the past, they avoid information on basic reproductive health unless when faced with a serious health challenge. At times, information on reproductive health is very scantily available to young people, so even those who want to know more do not have access to it, except when they have the opportunity to attend enlightenment workshops. If we must catch them young, then we must spread the information they need to the schools and colleges so they can make informed decisions when faced with dilemmas.

Poverty and Unemployment

The greatest weapon to subdue a people remains poverty. According to the United Nations General Assembly Session Declaration of Commitment on HIV/AIDS (2001), "The continued spread of poverty has the potential of hindering the realization of many of the Millennium Development Goals and deepen poverty in most of the world's population where the virus is prevalent."[30] Poverty is a consequence of unemployment. Unfortunately in Africa, the majority of those in the unemployed bracket are young people. In Europe, many young people would have started to fend for themselves between the ages of sixteen and eighteen years with support from government, but the same cannot be said of African youths, who still live with their parents at age thirty-five. The independence young people get early in life gives them an edge in the future to plan better once they are employed. But what we see today is the lack of basic infrastructure that will encourage job creation. So it's little wonder that many African governments are struggling in the twenty-first century to empower their young people to break the poverty circle they may have known over the years. This has being attributed to poor programme

---

[30]   United Nations report on HIV/AIDS, New York, 2001.

implementation and the corruption that has bedeviled the region for so long.

The more the gap of poverty increases in our society, the more social unrest we experience daily, since those who are supposed to be in productive areas are idle. Young people will have little or no choice but to resort to crimes like robbery, kidnapping, prostitution, etc., to make ends meet. This is normally what leads them to bad associations, and then all caution is thrown to the wind.

Young People Are Very Active

Most young people have latent energy that, if not properly directed toward positive causes, will surely be expended negatively. Young people are sexualized by the Internet, advertisements, and inappropriate movies shown at certain times of the day. When they are not properly guided, they prefer to stick to those negative influences. This drives them to experiment because they tend to be idle most of the time. Very few young people believe that sex is worth waiting for, because they see the opposite every day in society; as such, they want to lose their virginity as soon as the opportunity arises. The 2007 National HIV/AIDS Reproductive Health Survey showed that 15.7 percent of females under fifteen in Nigeria have had sex at one time or another with more than one male partner. This goes to show how we must create safeguards for our young people who are experiencing confusion about their reproductive health.

Peer Group Influence

Another reason young people are vulnerable is because of the associations they keep. Aristotle once said that we are social animals and that, as human beings, we always want to fraternize with others. Young people enjoy the company of their peers, but unfortunately it is not possible for all of them to hold the same values because they all come from different backgrounds. In the process of interacting, they often find themselves fraternizing with those who may hold negative or subjective opinions about many things, and those with bad habits quickly influence those with good habits. Sometimes, because some parents are not close to their children or wards, they find it difficult to confide in them or elders when challenged with health matters. Instead, they prefer to go to their peers, who more often than not have little or no knowledge themselves. As a result of this association, they make uninformed decisions that may jeopardize their future.

Stigmatization among Peers

Young people also fear stigmatization more than any group, so when they contract any STDs, they hide it rather than confide in somebody or seek medical help. Once a youth believes other family members will find out, they will carry those diseases with them for long periods of time before seeking treatment. Society itself, particularly in Africa, highly stigmatizes those with HIV, and young people do not want to experience the kind of stigmatization where family members and friends avoid them.

Lack of Counseling Centers

Another contributing factor to why young people can be vulnerable is a lack of easily accessible counseling centers. Young people find it difficult to travel long distances when challenged with their health, and that is why government will need to provide information to schools, so that these young people know where they can access information and seek the right counseling in confidence and, as much as possible, bring the right information to them regularly in their schools.

Lack of Good Mentors and Role Models in the Community

If young people do not have mentors and good role models to look up to in the community, it can become difficult for them to find somebody they can trust if they contract HIV or any other STDs. They are also more likely to hide it from their parents and family members unless they go through proper counseling. But if there is a good mentorship project, like an organization with a mentorship programme, in place for young people in and out of school, these young people will have people to trust and access whenever they experience health challenges.

Inadequate Provisions for an E-learning Environment

In times past, it was possible to go to a library and borrow books you ordinarily might not have been able to buy and to use its facilities. Now it is practically impossible to find functional public libraries in both communities and public schools in Africa. As a result, young people cannot even access information they would ordinarily have if newspapers, magazines, and Internet facilities were provided. If they were available, this would give them access to relevant information regarding their reproductive health without having to pay for it. These days you might find libraries in private schools that alienate others from poor backgrounds who cannot afford to attend. But having access to these basic facilities is more of a fundamental right than a privilege.

6.4. Common Symptoms of HIV/AIDS

- Feverish conditions all the time
- Whitish tongue
- Diarrhea
- Unstoppable cough
- Rashes on the body
- Constant weight loss without any reason

6.5. How HIV/AIDS Can Be Contracted

- Having unprotected sex with an HIV-infected person
- Keeping multiple sex partners
- Receiving HIV-infected blood through transfusion
- Sharing needles and other sharp instruments with infected persons
- Negative beliefs about the existence of HIV
- Untreated sexually transmitted disease (e.g., gonorrhea, syphilis, etc.)

6.6. What to Do If Infected with HIV/AIDS

- Consult a voluntary test center (VCT) located near you.
- Seek proper medical attention from a doctor.
- Share your HIV status with your partner or those you trust.
- Attend a counseling workshop.
- Begin proper medication (i.e., antiretroviral drugs).
- Eat well and avoid stressful conditions.
- Live a positive lifestyle.

6.7. How to Avoid Contracting HIV/AIDS

- Abstain from premarital and illicit sex.
- Avoid sharing the same sharp objects (e.g., blades, scissors, clippers, and syringes) with other people.
- Avoid using untreated blood for blood transfusions.
- Always wear gloves when caring for an infected person or helping a seriously injured accident victim.
- Use condoms consistently and correctly with sex partners.
- Remind oneself that condom does fail can save oneself. This is premised on the fact that condoms can fail and if it does during intercourse with an infected sex partner, the tendency to contract the disease becomes higher.
- Enlighten yourself and update your knowledge of HIV infection.

6.8. Positive Attributes towards People Living with HIV/AIDS (PLWHA)

- Don't stigmatize or discriminate against them.
- Avoid criticizing them and respect their rights.
- Show that you care about and love them.
- Encourage them to eat well and take their medications.
- Enlighten them on how to manage the disease.
- Support them in living a positive lifestyle.
- Encourage them to participate in every decision-making process that involves them.
- Encourage them to read and share information about their health with fellow PLWHAs.

6.9. Conclusion

The effect of HIV/AIDS on young people cannot be overemphasized or underestimated given the fact that this disease is spreading increasingly among youths, whose tendency to experiment with sex, even at an adolescent age, is very high.

Not only is HIV a deadly disease, but the mention of an HIV test sends shivers down the spines of many young people. Many of them shy away from taking the test, erroneously believing that the test result may turn them HIV-positive, and this fear of the unknown continues to keep many living in fear of the disease. From my experience watching those living positively with the disease, I have come to realize that it is better to know your status early because that will make you more careful and disciplined about your sexuality. In fact, it may increase your desire to settle down with one partner early.

Hepatitis B is another common disease among young people. Many young people carry the disease without actually knowing it, particularly drug addicts who are in the habit of sharing needles and syringes. HIV, just like other diseases such as cancer, can be terminal, but when it is detected early before it becomes full-blown AIDS), it can still be manageable. Research has shown that people can live positively with HIV and have normal lives. They can even have children without passing the virus to them and live for many years without anyone knowing they carry the virus thanks to advancements in science and medicine. With a high number of youths abusing hard drugs, the risk of contracting these diseases gets higher, especially among young addicts in the habit of sharing syringes and having multiple sex partners. Although HIV/AIDS can be contracted through ways other than sex, research has shown that the majority of young people are infected after unprotected sex.

To readdress this problem, parents should, as a matter of responsibility, educate their children and wards right from their teenage years about the various ways this disease can be contracted, because there have been instances when innocent children have been infected through sharing sharp objects with older people when they happened to be in their care. The conservative opinion in Africa that talking to young people about sex is taboo can no longer hold water because the youths of today get information fast, particularly from their peers, the Internet, and watching adults when they fool around. Most of the time, young people get the wrong information and impressions. They are eager to experiment with sex even as young as age ten, depending on the environment they are exposed to. Many young people, particularly those in Europe, are exposed to many sexual images and bombarded with sexual advertisements, so it's little wonder that those things quickly register in their minds. The next thing you know, they are ready to experiment. It is only commonsensical for it to happen. This is partly why there is a high level of teenage pregnancy among young people in Europe, with Britain having its fair share of the population of teenage mothers who are not prepared for family life. While it may not be wise to criminalize teenage pregnancy completely, it calls for serious concern because of the risk of contracting HIV, which they are often exposed to because they normally do not use the proper protection during intercourse despite the information available to them, nor are they willing to go for a test. In fact, when some young people are diagnosed with HIV, they end up running away instead of beginning treatment.

But in Africa one is more likely to see young people between the ages of twelve and fourteen experimenting with sex, depending on the age they begin to experience puberty, even though it's frowned upon and met with stiffer punishment due to the influence of cultural and religious values. Those who dare cross the line and get pregnant in their teenage years are strongly stigmatized and branded as good for nothing. Therefore, it is better for these young people to get the right advice about their sexuality from parents, guardians, or mentors once they are old enough and sensitive to their sexuality.

The view on teenage pregnancy is that it should not be criminalized, as is often done in Africa, where some pregnant teenage girls are abandoned by their families with little or no support. In Britain, reports suggest a significant rise in the number of teenage mothers, and people tend to look down on them rather than offer them support or advise on where they can get help, as if the problem is entirely theirs. To reduce this, teenage girls need to be given the right education and support to make informed decisions if they choose to experiment with sex. But they must be guided to practice abstinence from sex as teenagers, as this remains the best option regardless of the attraction to the opposite sex.

Youths have a duty, not only to themselves but to their family and society, to seek information about these diseases and safeguard their health by going online and reading information, readjusting their attitudes, and adopting more positive behavior towards sexuality and reproductive health to guarantee a healthy future.

Chapter 7

Youths and Drug Abuse

Most men would rather die, than think. Many do.

—Bertrand Russell

D rug abuse is a common phenomenon in today's society, and we need not look far to see it. The effect is glaringly obvious on users and traffickers. For some it has become a source of livelihood despite international efforts to stem the trade; others have become psychological dependent on the drugs that have become a part of their lives.

The history of drug abuse is as old as the existence of mankind, but it only gained prominence in more recent times when the impact became a social menace.

Recent statistics from the 2012 United Nations *World Drug Report* indicate that about 3.4 percent and 6.6 percent of the adult population ages fifteen to sixty-four still abuse illicit drugs including cannabis and amphetamine-type stimulants and excluding ecstasy, a commonly abused drug in the world today.[31] It proves the belief that a large percentage of youths, including secondary school and university students, are

---

[31]   United Nations, *World Drug Report*, 2012.

involved in drug abuse despite efforts to discourage them from taking hard drugs.

Again, it has been reported that the most common drug abused is marijuana (also known as cannabis), popularly called "igbo" or "weed" in local Nigerian parlance, with Africa maintaining 7.7 percent of the population of abusers and Nigeria following South Africa and Tanzania in cannabis seizure. According to the United Nations drug report (2012), "Cannabis is the largest illicit drug market by far and its size is one of its most important characteristics. Its consumer market is large, roughly 160 million people; its production centres are widely dispersed, existing in almost every country of the world, and its factors of production can be both flexible, rudimentary and small scale and permanent, highly technical and large scale (UN *World Drug Report* 2012)."

Many youths graduate from smoking cigarettes to trying Indian hemp mostly by association. Once cultivated, this habit is hard to drop despite the risk attached to it. Drug abuse has been found to typically result in inappropriate behaviour among abusers or addicts.

Furthermore, some psychologists have observed that when young people indulge in hard substances such as Indian hemp, it interferes with their learning by impairing their thinking faculties, which means they will no longer remember whatever they have learned. It can also change their sense of time, reduce concentration, and heavily distort coordination. Long-term dependence on this substance has been considered to affect productive activities and relationships, thereby resulting in psychological dependence.

Although the smoking of Indian hemp has been traced to lung cancer, respiratory problems, and early death in young people, young people still indulge in it.

As we know, youths are a very vulnerable set of people who are easily influenced by peer group activities and prone to risky behaviour. This is why Hamid Ghodse (1995) puts it thus: "As drug abuse spreads throughout the world, the target population is definitely the youths."[32]

It is for this reason that consistent effort must be stepped up by all stakeholders to apply preventive initiatives that will discourage youths from getting addicted to hard drugs, and stringent regulation should always be sustained in regulating the use of such substances.

7.1. What Is Drug Abuse?

Drug abuse and addiction have continued to generate lots of discussion globally among psychologists, social workers, and medical practitioners. Specialists differ on the level of drug intake that can be termed as abuse because in some societies some level of consumption of these substances is still permitted.

Social learning theorists ascribe drug abuse to societal influence, pointing out that "drug addiction is socially acquired."[33] For them, young people acquire it through an observatory, learning, and interaction process either with their peers or parents. Observing others who use these hard drugs and the effect they immediately produce induces their own craving for such drugs. Social learning theorists also posited that addictive behaviours are influenced by the

---

[32] Hamid Ghodse. *Drugs and Addictive Behaviour: A Guide to Treatment* (London: Blackwell Science Publishers, 1995), 70.

[33] James G. Barber. *Social Work with Addictions*, 3rd ed. (New York: Palgrave Macmillan Publishers, 2002), 20.

state of the user who may be trying to find cover for his or her stressful condition. "The drinker or drug taker is trying to master, tolerate, or reduce stressful internal or external demands."[34]

Psychologists like Abraham Wilker (1965) view addiction as 'the product of operant conditioning.' For him the 'drug addiction exhibited is a result of interaction of primary and secondary forces which creates a lifestyle of addiction for the addict. As he tries to reduce his level of intake, he tends to take it more and more without succeeding in stopping it."[35]

Macdonald (1965) viewed drug abuse as "a consequence of frustrated yearnings to be accepted by the society."[36] Firestone (1964) views drug abuse as 'a means of maximal differentiation of their peer group subculture from the values of the achieving society.'[37]

Sociobiologists have said that drug abuse can be explained by both the sociological and biological composition of the individual. These two components, which exist in an individual, tend to explain why people continually get addicted to hard drugs.

Moreover, the social workers in England have viewed it from a dual perspective of personal (behavioral) and environmental viewpoints. The World Health Organization (WHO), however, has given a more comprehensive definition

34 James G. Barber. *Social Work with Addictions*, 3rd ed. (New York: Palgrave Macmillan Publishers, 2002), 23.

35 James G. Barber. *Social Work with Addictions*, 3rd ed. (New York: Palgrave Macmillan Publishers, 2002).20

36 James G. Barber. *Social Work with Addictions*, 3rd ed. (New York: Palgrave Macmillan Publishers, 2002), 41.

37 James G. Barber. *Social Work with Addictions*, 3rd ed. (New York: Palgrave Macmillan Publishers, 2002), 41.

on drug abuse by describing it as thus: "A state, psychic and sometimes physical, resulting from the interaction between a living organism and a drug characterized by behavioral and other responses that always include a compulsion to take drugs on a continuous or periodic basis in order to experience psychic effects and sometimes to avoid the discomfort of its absence. Tolerance may or may not be present." [38]

This definition appears to embrace most definitions of the past, except it does not appear to take into perspective individual will of the abuser.

In my research, I have been able to deduce that those who take hard drugs do it as a matter of free will, thereby exercising their freedom to choose. Abusing drugs is a willful decision by the abuser who, in an attempt to achieve a psychic state of being that he or she may not be able to achieve by ordinary means, resorts to abusing substances that can guarantee such a momentous state on a continual basis.

Axel Klein rightly observes and agrees to this position in his own writing: "In most instances of initiation, however, the user takes the drug voluntarily, knowing that it is risky. Usually instigated by friends and siblings, drug initiations form core experiences of identity development and social bonding."[39]

Thus, we can safely conclude there is always a personal gain attached to taking hard drugs, and if they didn't believe this, they could have acted otherwise.

---

[38] Hamid Ghodse. *Drugs and Addictive Behaviour: A Guide to Treatment* (London: Blackwell Science Publishers, 1995), 70.

[39] Axel Klein. *Drugs and the World* (London: Reaktion Books Ltd., 2008), 31.

However, there are other youths whose friends indulge in hard drugs, yet they refuse to be influenced by such behavior. This is why Axel Klein maintained further that "during initiation, drug use is not an automatic impulse or an involuntary response but the outcome of a rational and voluntary decision making process."[40] This, however, proves that not all youths are pushed into it when they fraternize with others their age, though this is only in the minority. The best bet has always been to avoid those groups of friends if you don't want to begin the habit of smoking marijuana.

Although some psychologists have maintained that those who abuse drugs do so because they suffer from personality disorders, we have seen many cases of young people who are told smoking marijuana is a prerequisite to be admitted into certain groups. These youths do not suffer from personality disorders of any kind. This leads us to believe that more youths indulge in it out of their will. It's simply a matter of choice.

7.2. The Place of Drug Abuse among Nigerian Youths

There is no doubt that substance abuse among youths, particularly in Nigeria, has continued unabated, thereby creating a huge social problem because the users have now become a burden to the society and to their families.

People prefer to call those who take Indian hemp "area boys" in local language, but according to recent research, it is not only the deviants who abuse drugs; politicians, the young, and upwardly mobile people who want to climb

---

[40]   Ibid, 32.

in social circles abuse it with impunity. Indian hemp and alcohol remain the most abused.

The reason that Indian hemp has been readily available is because it is still being grown everywhere, particularly in parts of the southwest. It is very cheap, readily available to youths, and not well regulated. When you visit certain public centres meant for recreation and abandoned buildings in major cities like Lagos, for instance, it is common to find groups of young people smoking Indian hemp freely. No one can challenge them except the law enforcement agents. Even when the hemp smokers are arrested, they are quickly freed and return back to their trade despite the danger they pose to themselves and to other members of the society.

The abuse of these substances has permeated secondary schools and colleges, because the use of marijuana has become popular among students. In the past, it was hard to find secondary school students in the trade, but now it is common to find them in association with drug addicts. Smoking marijuana was apparently popularised when the late famous Afro beat musician, Fela Anikulapo Kuti, glamorised smoking "cannabis" on stage while performing in his shrine and encouraged his followers to use it. This is why, even at the African Shrine and other public spaces, you are likely to find many young people still smoking weed around the shrine without consideration for the health risk it poses to themselves and others. In the course of research I conducted in 2009, I posed several questions to young people to find out why they used the controlled substance. Some respondents gave reasons such as "It is good for the mind to be able to think clearly" or "It is good for growing of the hair." Others said it helped them "not to bother about their problems" or "to contemplate and be in a sober mood." One major fact is that they are conscious of the decision to abuse drugs and the risk it poses to their health. Yet others may point to their role models and argue that lot of artistes, like the late Fela Anikulapo Kuti, Bob Marley, and others, used it and it didn't kill them. Thus, they don't actually see the risk it poses to their lives. No doubt, many of today's Youths abuse drugs in one form or the other, but the abuse of alcohol has also been argued to have a correlation with the abuse of hard drugs. In other words, youths who abuse alcohol regularly are likely to also abuse drugs, and the combination is very detrimental to their health.

The National Drug Law Enforcement Agency (NDLEA) was set up to control and arrest the drug problem after it became obvious that the police could not handle the situation alone to break the supply chain, as Nigeria was becoming a transit zone. But as is the case with other policies and implementation, the agency has been plagued by corruption, inefficiency, and political interference, thereby limiting their ability to successfully fight the supply network. Consequently, the NDLEA has been unable to implement a demand reduction strategy.

Most efforts put in place to keep youths from abusing drugs have not been effective, and that accounts for why the battle is being lost daily. The resultant effect is high level of crime among the youth population and more destitution on our streets.

7.3. Contributing Factors to Youth Abuse of Hard Drugs

Many scholars have argued in support of the existing relationship between the environmental influence and drug addiction, but there has not been a comprehensive consensus that environmental influence is the main factor for people abusing drugs. Therefore, accepting that position alone will ignore other salient factors. Here are some contributing factors that should be considered, in my opinion, as to why youths are prone to drug addiction, but that is not to say there is a direct causal link. Suffice it to say, the prevalence of these factors does encourage and influence the multitude of youths into drug addiction or abuse.

Social Lifestyle

The social lifestyle in today's world is highly sophisticated and dynamic, particularly in this global age. Thus, there is only a thin line between what is morally right and what is not. Put differently, our society has become permissive of all kinds of viciousness and lifestyles, departing sharply from what common sense can accommodate. In fact, Nigerian youths are worst hit because of the influences pouring in from Western culture, such as taking hard drugs now being considered a part of life. Moreover, they are not able to decide whether this pattern of life may lead them to ruin or not. Because of their vulnerability and lack of good role models, they are always quick to embrace new culture no matter how risky such actions are.

Influence of Peer Groups

Man is a social animal, as Aristotle once opined. This means that most youths will always seek out and associate with their peers. It is in this process of interaction that many become influenced by the negative lifestyle of drug addicts. In some cases they take hard drugs to belong with those groups, and it is also to prove they can belong, too, because this is what may make the members open up to them. This has become one of the commonest ways that youths come in first contact with hard drugs, and immediately they begin to achieve a psychic state. They become hooked on these drugs before they know it.

Anxiety and Depression

Youths who suffer from anxiety and depression, whether caused by relationship breakdown, job loss, years of unemployment, family challenges, loss of a loved one, or desire to escape from problems, are more likely to take hard drugs.

Promise of False Security

Hard drugs sometimes give people false security because, during that psychic state, they often believe that problems they are trying to avoid don't exist, forgetting that the altered state provides only temporary relief from them. To achieve a constant relief from those issues, they continue to abuse these drugs. This is what normally leads to dependency.

Breakdown of the Family System

The family was meant to be the bedrock of the society, which is supposed to mirror the society where young people exist. There cannot be a well-ordered society without a stable and cohesive family system. Unfortunately, today in Nigeria, the family system has gradually lost its roots and is fast becoming more Eurocentric in nature with its deep, individualistic tendencies, which is in contrast with the traditional communal family system African was known for. This may account for why a divorce card is flashed at the slightest provocation these days, and the children suffer more when such a split occurs. I believe we are given the duty by God to maintain the family system. He ordained it to be so to keep order in the society. Therefore, when we begin to amend or cause cosmetic changes to the structure of the family, the system is distorted from its original purpose as designed right from creation. By accommodating such abnormalities, like same-sex marriages and high divorce rates, in the community, families not only fail in their duty towards their children but create chaos and confusion that their children will inherit. Those children are not able to appreciate the values and need for a family unit, so it's little wonder those who are quick to get divorced are young, misguided people. This is why youths who grow up under such family circumstances easily resort to drug abuse when depressed or faced with life challenges without the support mechanism of the family to guide them in the right direction.

Unemployment

Unemployment has become a tear in the flesh of government policies in Nigeria because it has defied many policies initiated to control it. Unemployment is not exclusive to Nigeria or Africa; in fact, with the present level of global recession, most industrialised countries have had their fair share of the problem. The only difference is that countries like Nigeria and other developing countries in Africa are especially hard hit because of their weak industrial base and low investment capacity, thereby making the issue of unemployment difficult to tackle. Unemployment has remained one major factor that drives youths to antisocial behaviour and use of hard drugs. When they are unable to find something to do, the tendency is always there to find peers with similar interests, so the inclination to experiment with hard drugs becomes very high. And that is when you see young people gather at public parks, abandoned sites, and other hidden places to use these drugs.

Financial Challenges

Many youths, particularly in Africa, are poor either because of unemployment or because they lack the financial independence to develop themselves, and so they always have to fall back on parents, siblings, or relatives. When it comes to getting money for illicit drugs, they often resort to crime. They know it will be difficult to cultivate such habits by depending on their family for financial support. Therefore, young people take refuge in hard drugs to escape the reality of the financial challenges confronting them. The belief among such drug-dependent youths is that they will find succour in using those drugs rather than thinking out a constructive means of overcoming the problem itself. Still others who use drugs also trade or sell them because it is seen as a very lucrative business.

Low Parental Care, Affection, and Guidance

Parents, who because of the influence of cosmopolitan life fail in their responsibility of caring and giving affection to their children and wards, stand the risk of pushing them into the use of hard drugs. Many young people who have indulged in drug use have been found to carry a heavy burden of one family challenge or another, which they find hard to overcome. Some have problems communicating with their parents because they are not given the chance to express themselves, and this often drives them out of the home as they seek affection from peer groups who share their interests. They not only listen to them but give them misguided advice, which they follow most of the time. Unfortunately, some parents, who both have to work to keep the family going, fail to balance the needs of the family with their careers. Building a career is often given top priority by those parents as opposed to building a good home for the children; hence, they resort to shifting parental roles to close relatives, maids, and neighbours.

Low Self-esteem

Some youths suffer from low self-esteem and think they are inferior when they are in certain circles. When they are unable to overcome this inferiority complex, some of them use hard drugs to boost their mental state to be able to interact in those circles. Hard drugs give them a psychic state of false self-esteem, which they now depend on to express themselves. This is why some artistes take drugs before they can face an audience to perform.

7.4. Challenges of Eradicating Drug Abuse among Youths in Nigeria

Lack of Proper Implementation of Policies

Poor implementation of policies, no matter how good the intention, has become the bane of our policy performance. In fact, sometimes the policy is defeated even before it is implemented, as if it was developed to fail. In many instances we have seen how good policies are poorly implemented due to poor regulatory practice or lack of regulatory framework to support such policy success. For instance, when the National Youth Development Policy of 2001 was instituted, all levels of government were assigned their responsibilities regarding funding of youth programmes. But in practice, the lower levels of government, like the local government, hardly discharges its own responsibility to the various youth organisations under their territory; instead, these organisations always go out of their way to borrow money to fund their developmental needs when provisions have been made in their annual budgets. This kind of practice has stifled youth development activities in most local governments. More often than not, it puts the young people at loggerheads with their local councils and elected officials when budgeted funds for youth programmes do not get to the primary beneficiaries. In light of this situation, it's practically difficult for youth workers and volunteers to succeed in carrying out local development programmes that should have engaged the youths.

Prevalence of Poverty among Our Youths

The youths are poor not only because they lack access to job opportunities, but because they are not empowered. This had made them very vulnerable to crime and antisocial behaviour. Because many of the unskilled youths don't have access to entrepreneurial programmes, it is little wonder they take solace in dealing drugs because this provides them a means to earn a living. This calls for the provision of entrepreneurial programmes instituted at all local levels, so these youths who don't have access to educations can still have opportunities for training in their field of interest. In past administrations poverty-related programmes were instituted, such as the Better Life for Rural Women, Family Support Programme, etc. Such poverty programmes failed, however, because they were not implemented across the board and the implementation was largely flawed. Therefore, it's expedient to have a more sustained comprehensive programme that will not be affected by change in government. The issue of localising it cannot be overemphasised.

Protection of Supplier Chains by Government and Law Enforcement Agencies

The supply chain of drugs to the market has continued largely because of the tolerant policies against offenders and collusion with law enforcement agencies. The protection drug traffickers and supply chains enjoy from some law enforcement agencies has become the greatest hindrance to the reduction of drugs on our streets. Although government agencies like the Nigerian Drug Law Enforcement Agency (NDLEA) confiscate hard drugs on a regular basis, the sincerity of the process is seriously in question because professionalism is sacrificed daily on the altar of greed, and endemic corruption has become second nature.

Poorly Funded Enlightenment and Poorly Directed Programmes

When programmes are formulated for execution, one of the major drawbacks of the successful implementation of such programmes has always been poor or epileptic release of funds. This problem can only be corrected by legislation so that people in authority can be held responsible if their actions contradict the implementation process of the programme. Many times, funds meant for enlightenment programmes are diverted to other causes or siphoned into private pockets. There is no doubt that prevention techniques has always proven to be more effective in reducing the number of young people taking to drug addiction, so if the programmes meant to reduce this number are poorly directed, the results are going to be insignificant. For this reason there has to be an increase in this direction especially because the drug trade is becoming so sophisticated today. The focus of the enlightenment programme should go beyond rhetoric and focus on the essentials, tackling the issue of drug addiction.

Lack of Social Welfare Policies for Unemployed Youths

In a country like ours where unemployment is a common problem and no white-collar jobs are available for graduates, there is a need to enact a law providing social benefits for those unemployed on a government database, where information can be expediently shared between the government and employers of labour. Although it has been argued in several quarters that corruption may wipe off the shine and benefits of such a programme, and that enacting such a law creates a larger concentration of youths in the unemployment net, the absence of such a programme highly increases the level of crime and insecurity. Every country has its own share of welfare benefit thieves. Therefore, for us to succeed in ours, we must learn from other countries' mistakes and adopt a system of welfare benefits that can be easily tracked. While we may not guarantee that there will be full-proof technology, we can manage this system to keep benefit thieves at a manageable level.

Non-existence of a Comprehensive Data on Traffickers and Addicts

In a country like ours where statistical information is not adequately taken into consideration, either because it's not existent or it's practically relegated in decision-making processes, the resultant effect relies more on subjective judgement, which has not proven to be effective in finding solutions to these social challenges. Therefore, it is not surprising that government agencies and departments don't have functional research and development units that would have been saddled with this responsibility. This is why it is difficult most of the time for researchers to access adequate data on the usage of hard drugs among youths and measure performance of policies set out to tackle the situation.

Inadequate Data on Youth Population

The effectiveness of every policy that targets youth depends partly on the demographic data on the youth population in a census. Unfortunately, any census conducted is either inaccurate or too politically influenced to be considered reliable as a tool for decision-making. As a result, it is impractical for the policies set in this sector to measure up to the actual problem, because a lot of underestimation would have been assumed.

High Level of Unemployment

The high level of unemployment in the teeming population of youths, whether skilled or unskilled, is a very big challenge for any government. In view of the present recession in Europe and other parts of the world, youths are hit worse than any demographic. This is because the companies are trimming down their labour forces due to losses. They do not have the capacity to hire the younger ones that are just graduating from school. Aside from that, they may be receiving inadequate financial support from their parents, making them a prime target for drug users and traffickers. It is no longer common like it was in the early '60s and '70s to see a job waiting for one after going through the rigors of university training. It is for this reason that attention must shift from white-collar job training to an entrepreneurial education that teaches life support skills. This way, youths don't come out of school looking for jobs, but they create jobs for the unskilled given the right climate. For instance, have secondary students attend a five-hour-per-week class on how to become an entrepreneur along with their regular classes, establish a charity organization with mentors who have succeeded in such ventures, volunteer, or take up part-time jobs to teach these subjects rather than glorifying some traditional courses.

Non-existence of a Comprehensive Rehabilitation Programme for Drug Addicts

No comprehensive policy that guides the rehabilitation of drug addicts is another challenge when attempting to control youth drug abuse. Once youths are discharged from their treatment, they are often left on their own to begin again, which is very difficult in a society like ours that discriminates seriously against ex-addicts. This is made even worse when some companies refuse to hire them for jobs because of their past. Although many non-governmental organisations are directly involved in the rehabilitation of these ex-addicts, having a broad policy framework that will spell out roles and guidelines for the government agencies or any organisation doing rehabilitation is essential, if we want to be certain these youths are not discriminated against.

Moribund Laws That Are Not in Tune with Reality

We cannot underestimate the importance of having our laws updated and in tune with reality if we want to salvage the present situation. For instance, it is disheartening to see that the laws, which ordinarily give more power to the youth in their own affairs than the political class, oppress advocacy among youth leaders. In practice, advocacy in whatever form should be guaranteed and protected by law rather than the criminalising of those who dare to blow the whistle when a policy is wrongly implemented. The failure to regularly improve these laws not only sparks conflict and creates a lacuna but kills the interest of those youths who would ordinarily be engaged in these programmes.

Inadequate Funding of Preventative Initiatives

The old maxim that says prevention is better than cure still holds water when tackling youth vices. No country that fails to adequately provide for preventive initiatives ever achieves success in crime reduction. The problem has always been that government alone is expected to pay for this, but in practice it doesn't work. This is why adequate policy framework is highly desired to create the groundwork for which other participants, like the organised private sector or high net-worth individuals who desire to sacrifice their resources, can contribute to youth development. A relief package can come in the form of tax rebates, exemption from certain categories of import tax, company tax, etc. This can only be achieved through wide consultation with all stakeholders, which eventually leads to legislation. There is no doubt that such a policy would be firmly rooted because it was widely discussed across the board. For this policy to be become sustainable, its outcome should be measured yearly. The consultation may take time to complete, but with a target set the present situation of having to use fire brigade funding would be a thing of the past for youth development programmes.

Glorification of Popular Artistes or Celebrities Who Abuse Drugs

The way the society glorifies celebrities who use drugs negatively affects the attempt to reduce youth drug use. The society mirrors the culture of a people, and to counter this there is an expedient need for youth mentorship programmes in organisations working with young people, especially where only celebrities are supposed to be positive role models, to give mentoring classes on a volunteer basis.

7.5. Effects of Drug Abuse among Youths

1. Poor health
2. Poor productivity
3. Overconcentration of budget on social welfare institutions at the expense of other developmental needs
4. Decreased labour force
5. Low gross domestic product
6. High unemployment and underemployment
7. Increased crime rates and other social vices
8. Underutilisation of sport and recreational resources
9. High rate of school dropouts
10. Increased illicit sex among youths, which can lead to teenage pregnancy and increased incidence of STDs
11. Contracting HIV by sharing syringes with drug addicts

7.6. Practical Initiatives to Reduce Drug Abuse among Youths

1. Constant education and properly directed enlightenment programmes
2. Provision of rehabilitative programmes for addicts
3. Creation of more skill acquisition centres for youths
4. Availability of free treatment drugs
5. Family counselling for the addict's family
6. Regular training on harm reduction technique for medical personnel responsible for prescribing drugs
7. Adequate funding of preventive initiatives
8. Encouraging sporting and outdoor activities through the provision of more sports centres in every local community
9. Legal provision allowing rehabilitated drug addicts to enjoy certain social benefits until they can find gainful employment
10. Creation of more employment opportunities for our youths
11. Involving youths in the decision making process
12. Establishment of antidrug abuse clubs in secondary schools
13. Empowerment of young people with entrepreneurial skills and training
14. Aggressive tackling of supply routes
15. Establishment of drug reduction units in departments that work with the youths
16. Creating a central database for youths

7.7. Conclusion

In Nigeria, where laws are broken with impunity and corruption takes a higher pedestal in the scheme of things, the resolve to tackle drug abuse and trafficking can be an uphill task. The findings in my research showed that many youths who abuse hard drugs are knowledgeable about the inherent danger that hard drugs pose to their health, because in their response 60 percent of the sampled population alluded to the fact that they are conscious of the danger. They feel strongly that youths should not be taking these substances, even though those still indulging in the habit don't consider it harmful enough to be discouraged from it. When youths were asked if they wanted drugs banned, 50 percent submitted that drugs should not be banned; only 16 percent agreed that they should be banned outright.

Nevertheless, we must not delude ourselves that the war can be won anytime, because society is changing fast and with it comes lifestyles that are not traditionally part of our culture. The fact that some narcotic substances are still allowed in some countries, and that youths act out of their freewill, leaves a hole in the global effort to stop the abuse of these substances.

Again, we live in a global village, and that allows youths to interact and associate freely while getting exposed to different influences that come their way. Added to that, youths see how drug use has become part of a social lifestyle in Europe and America as normally reflected in today's films and the culture of hip-hop viewed over the Internet. Youths who watch those movies and musical videos easily adopt, imitate, and stick to the culture they portray.

Mike Featherstone pointed this out when he said that "drug use no longer forms part of an alternative reward system for social dropouts, but is an aspect of a calculating hedonism where pleasure is integrated into the rhythm of work and life."[41]

That accounts for why the direction in our approach now shifts to adoption of harm reduction technique, which means rather than criminalising the users, our focus should shift towards reducing the harm it causes to users, potential abusers, and society. This can be achieved through regular education and adoption of proactive policies that will discourage or make it difficult for new entrants to embrace the drug culture while focusing on the cause and not the effect alone.

Again, we should attack the foundation of the belief that using hard drugs is part of a social lifestyle. Although smoking kills, youths don't believe anything bad will happen to them for a long time, so they will likely pick up the habit of smoking while attending secondary school.

In conclusion, governments and more non-governmental organisations must intensify the antidrug campaign, particularly for those teenagers who are yet to be bugged by the habit. Celebrity rehabilitees should also be allowed to share their stories with young people either in their schools, churches, mosques, or clubs. There is a growing adoption of the celebrity lifestyle, and young people look up to them. So when they fall, they are able to put their acts together through rehabilitation, and they become a veritable tool for drumming home this message to our youths who may be

---

[41] Mike Featherstone, Mike Hepworth, and Bryon S. Turner, eds. *The Body: Social Process and Cultural Theory* (London: Sage, 1990).

lured by drug barons into using and trafficking these drugs in the future.

Donor agencies and development partners should increase funding through trade to African governments to increase their capacity to track the drug traffickers and empower youths with entrepreneurial skill and initiatives.

But to effectively achieve the objective of reducing drug abuse among youths, there is an urgent need amongst others to establish drug reduction units in ministries responsible for social welfare and build more correctional facilities to rehabilitate drug addicts.

Chapter 8

Youths and Investment Clubs

Be fearful when the market is greedy and be greedy when the market is fearful.

—Warren Buffet

Many of our youths are poor today because they are not taught how to invest in their future from a very early age, and as a result, they end up spending all they have earned with nothing to show for it when they grow old. This is why it is a common feature to see aspiring young professionals jump on every consumer promotion rolled out by banks. Whether the interest pays them or not in the long run is hardly a thing to consider. All they want is to acquire and continually live under the burden of debt, so it's little wonder most young people still in their thirties depend on parents, some on sugar daddies or mummies, godfathers, and others to survive. They find it hard to get financial independence early in life. If you ask most youths which companies are the most capitalized in the Nigerian capital market, you'd hardly get 10 percent to give you the correct answer. They prefer to spend their monies on the latest computer games, phones, designer clothes, cars, and other material things that do not add value to their fortunes. It is true that youths cannot learn it from schools because financial intelligence is not included in school curricula; they can only learn it in the business and corporate world either by interaction, association, or reading.

Investment comes in different forms: stocks, real estate, bonds, futures, or commodities. Whatever type of investment one decides to go into depends largely on the amount of information and guidance one has or acquired through interaction with others involved in the market. There is no doubt the stock market remains a justifiable and reliable vehicle for accumulating wealth, but those who will play in it must acquire the necessary financial intelligence to succeed in the venture.

The stock market in Nigeria is still growing. Being an emerging market, it still guarantees a generous return on investment if investment is done over a long period of time. The market has its upside and downside, just like a swing that goes back and forth, and it is controlled by forces of demand and supply, although sometimes other artificial elements direct the order of the market.

The capital market is the place for raising long-term funds or doing long-term investing, where primarily the forces of demand and supply do operate.

Capital is one of the factors necessary for the production process to be complete. That accounts for the importance attached to the growth of the capital market, because this helps to redirect money away from the surplus sector to the deficit sector of the economy.

The capital market holds lots of opportunities for our young people. Youth clubs can take advantage of it by raising the needed funds to achieve their future dreams and projects.

This can be achieved by either investing as an individual or as a group. This is also advocated by Fox in his writing, *On Investing for Life*, when he posited that "the great thing about youth-run investment clubs is that it is a real adventure in learning how to obtain financial assets because for the first time in their life they are in control and they have an important decision to make either to spend or invest their money."

In addition to that, when youths invest in stocks, it helps them to do research into companies and follow market trends through financial publications such as newspapers, journals, and company reports, which in turn improves their reading and communication skills.

"Learning about the stock market could open doors to a host of highly paid occupations and it gives an insight into many career opportunities beyond the investment field."[42] But for the sake of this discourse, I'm going to concentrate more on collective investing in the stock market known as investment clubs.

Voluntary organizations, youth clubs, or youths themselves can form youth investment clubs to raise capital and invest in the capital market so that both profit and loss are collectively shared. Although this is a relatively new investment vehicle in this part of the world, in Europe and America it's a common thing to see youths come together to form a youth investment club where they can pool resources together to invest over a long period of time and increase their drive for financial knowledge. For instance, St. George's Episcopal Church in Washington, DC, started

---

[42]   Carolyn M. Brown. *The Millionaires' Club* (New York: John Wiley & Sons, 2000).

its youth investment in 1996 with only fifteen members and an initial investment of $750 contributed from the fifty-dollar membership dues. They were able to create a portfolio valued at over $25,000 in their first year of operation just by investing in growth stocks and reinvesting all dividends.[43]

8.1. Benefits of Investing in the Capital Market

Dividends

Investing in shares of companies, or bonds, automatically entitles one to earn profit in the form of dividends on one's investment. A dividend is an annual profit shared among all existing investors or bondholders in the registrar's book at the end of each financial year once it is declared. Therefore, every investor is entitled to a dividend's payout annually based on the units held by each investor upon declaration. Companies declare dividends only when they make profit, and that's why investors must be conscious of the companies they invest in so they can be assured of a good dividend payout yearly. One way to judge this is to look at the dividend history of that company, the ratio of payout over the years, and its current earnings per share before deciding to invest in that company.

Capital Appreciation

Another benefit for investing in the capital market is capital appreciation. The value of shares appreciates, and just like every form of investment in real estate, it also appreciates from the original price due to activities of demand and supply,

---

[43] Carolyn M. Brown. *The Millionaires' Club* (New York: John Wiley & Sons, 2000).

the company's profit margin, its earnings per share, and other factors that affect the pricing of that stock. Although capital appreciation is the largest factor that influences certain investors' decisions to invest in a particular form of investment, this should not be so, because experience has shown that speculators who invest for this reason alone can have their hands burnt if the market reacts negatively, in spite of the fundamentals of that particular stock.

Bonus or Script Issue

Another spectacular benefit of investing in the stock market is the opportunity to get additional shares added to one investment, referred to as bonus or script issue. In 2006, for instance, First Bank PLC declared a bonus of one for one, which implied that if before the date it was declared you had, say, 10,000 units of a certain stock, you would earn an additional 10,000 units, bringing your total holding to 20,000 units at the current market value. In 2007 the same bank declared another bonus of one for six, which implied for every six units of shares you possessed, you qualified for an extra one, bringing your total share holdings to 23,333 units at the end of the 2007 financial year. If the price remains up and doesn't come down significantly, it means you would have recovered your initial investment within a short period if you sell the initial units plus the bonus issue.

Ownership Ego

By investing in a company, you automatically become a shareholder and part owner of that company. This also guarantees you certain rights, such as the right to vote and be voted for to become a director in that company. You also have the right to attend general meetings and vote during extraordinary general meetings on issues, including bonuses, fixing of emoluments for directors, appointment of directors and audit committee, mergers and acquisition, split or reconstruction of shares, change in the company's capitalization, and any other decision that may require votes from time to time.

Liquidity

Daily share trading on the floor of the stock exchange gives investors an avenue to convert their shares to liquid form by selling it to get cash at any time. The market has been structured in such a way that with the application of the T+3 rule, meaning transaction day plus three days, investors can actually cash out within a week of placing the stocks on sale as long they are sold on the floor compared to real estate.

Collateral for Loans

Every shareholder can use his or her stocks as collateral for obtaining loans from any financial institution to fund new businesses or expand existing ones both in the short and long term. However, in the midst of a declining market and global recession, investors should be conscious of a bank's reluctance to advance credit based on shares as collateral alone.

8.2. How to Form Youth Investment Clubs

Youth investment clubs can be formed by youths who belong to the same clubs in colleges, tertiary institutions, or voluntary organizations that aspire to create wealth for their organization by coming together and registering such clubs as a cooperative, with mentors or advisers and a board of executives elected annually or biannually to manage affairs. But when forming youth investment clubs, consider the following seven factors:

1. Common purposes or objectives

Youths who come together to form an investment club must first consider if they share the same objective of coming to the capital market, because like minds think alike. At every stage of the investment plan, decisions will have to be reached collectively. That alone justifies why they must share a common purpose.

2. Clear-cut investment plans and objectives

Once youths have agreed to come together to form a youth investment club, they should determine what their objectives are. For instance, do they want to invest for long-term or short-term growth stock or income-generating stock, as this will practically determine the kind of investment to pool their resources into. There is no doubt that the best form is the long-term investment to achieve consistent and safe returns on investment. Many times, however, certain types of investments can be tailored for the short term depending on the opportunities available at the time. Also, there should be a clear-cut policy on dividend reinvestment plans and bonuses earned on the investment.

3. Selecting a broker

An investment club wanting to invest in any of the capital market instrument must employ the service of a stockbroker, who will manage the account on their behalf through a licensed stock brokerage company. "As a general rule there isn't anybody who is apt to be as well qualified to advise you about your investment as your broker."[44]

The choice of a broker should be based not on emotion or familiarity but on merit and the kind of service delivery. This is so because in many cases, the broker's level of financial market intelligence determines how well he or she is able to take advantage of the market for clients. There are other investment advisers and stock market agents licensed by the Chartered Institute of Stockbrokers (CIS) in Nigeria who are market analysts, portfolio managers, and have websites dedicated to market analysis and stock pick recommendations. They too can be consulted from time to time for a second opinion on the market or engaged on a part-time basis to offer market advisory services to the clubs at a minimal fee before major investment decisions are made.

4. Selection of executives

All investment clubs are time-consuming. As such, they require willing hands ready to sacrifice time to monitor the investments. Therefore, the financial secretary and treasurer should be carefully selected, because they will relate with the broker from time to time when submitting a buy or purchase mandate, payment of cheques, or collections. They should be signatories to the club account with the stock brokerage firm. They should only appoint credible members who understand common financial matters and who do not act based on their selfish interest by colluding with brokers to defraud the club. They should be people who are interested in assisting their members to gain foundational knowledge,

---

[44] Louise and Brendan Engel. *How to Buy Stocks*, 7th ed. (New York: Bantam Books, 1982), 215.

so that other youths coming after them can also take over in the future.

5. Funding of the investment
This is another factor that should be considered: whether they will want to fund the investment through monthly dues or a weekly contribution. But what matters is that there is a level playing field for all members to operate and that members pay an equal amount, because whatever profit is made is also shared equally. However, fines must be imposed on defaulters once a sum is agreed upon and be paid into the club's account to ensure that every member pays when due.

6. Bylaws
All investment clubs, like other clubs, are guided by bylaws. The same goes for every youth investment club to ensure the club's success and bring members in line with their responsibilities and rights.

7. Cost of investing
Before investing in any instrument, clubs should ensure they have idea of the cost of investing and do the mathematics with their broker on the average cost and expected returns over a period of time. In Nigeria capital market, due to the recession that has hit the market, charges have been reduced considerably to below 1.5 percent or less both during buying and selling. This alone is an incentive for a buyer to invest massively. Although no one can tell exactly the actual returns in the capital market since it's controlled by forces of supply and demand, but when investment is done over a long period of years, one can be guaranteed generous returns in form of rich dividends paid out, capital appreciation, and bonus

issue. In money market instruments, it's easier to calculate what accrues to a particular investment, but it's still good to look beyond the rhetoric of the bankers and focus more on the naira and kobo that will add up at the tenure of the investment after deducting their various legal and regulatory charges plus tax.

8.3. Strategies of Investing in the Capital Market

Create a Mixed Investment

Every investment club that wants to play in the capital market should not limit itself to shares. In fact, the club should, as a matter of policy, appropriate a certain percentage of its funds to shares, mutual funds, bonds, and fixed income instruments in the money market, such as treasury bills, fixed deposits, and other forms of liquid investment. This will help to hedge the organisation against any serious market drift.

Invest in Primary or Private Placements

Investment clubs should take advantage of primary offerings because they will normally come at a discount and with private placement are considered to have strong fundamentals for growth. We now know, due to the recent policy by the Nigerian Stock Exchange (NSE), to list all companies doing private placement on the floor at their private placement price, so we are unlikely to experience the usual surge in price upon the listing of the stock as was the case in 2007 and 2008.

In addition, current trends have revealed that "there exists a symmetric relationship between the primary and the secondary market, and that is why whenever companies are doing their public offering, the secondary market normally slows down due to lots of investors selling to partake in the offers, as was experienced in the Nigeria market in 2007"[45]

Therefore, during such a period investment clubs should always envisage such decline and sell a part of their holdings to take positions in those offers, especially private placements with growth prospects, after a careful research of the offer and its future prospects, because upon listing there's likely going to be a pool of activities around that company's shares. It may continue to attract investor's attention for some time, particularly if the company has a good corporate governance policy and it's a growth stock.

Use Your Own Club's Funds

Most of the time clubs are tempted to borrow funds like individuals and invest massively in the market, especially if the market experiences a bullish run as was the case in the Nigerian market between 2006 and the first quarter of 2008. However, it's always better to begin with your own contributions and grow them over a period of time. The Nigerian capital market, being an unpredictable and volatile market (unlike European markets, which can be predictably stable), requires clubs use less borrowed funds unless those funds can be acquired at a very low cost and be available for a long time. In a declining market, it is not advisable to go borrowing as some investors would do, particularly as interest rates will usually be increased by the apex bank in order to mop up excessive cash in the system and stabilise

---

[45] Matthew O. Dominic. "Investing in a Bearish Market: Strategies to Adopt." http://bizcovering.com/investing/investing-in-a-nigerian-bear-market-strategies-to-adopt.

an inflation-ridden economy like ours. Besides that, this will definitely increase the cost of investing in the secondary market and rub off on the profit to be made. The sure bet has always been to keep to what you already have in your kitty and review your portfolio regularly so as not to record more losses in case the market dips further, as was recently experienced in the Nigerian capital market from the second through fourth quarters of 2008. During this period clubs can move some of their funds into money market instruments pending the stability of the equity market, but exiting completely could be fatal to the health of their investment.

Regular Review of Your Portfolio

There is no gain in keeping shares in your portfolio that cannot recover what you have lost in a declining period, or buying shares and keeping them for so long even when you have gained capital appreciation on them, unless your objective is strictly for a stable income. However, sometimes a bullish market can turn bearish, and every individual or organisation that plays in the capital market should always envisage this because every market has its own life cycle of profit and loss. In such cases, it is best to review your portfolio by selling all nonperforming stocks before they lose 50 percent of their value and reinvest them in shares with strong fundamentals that may have lost 50 percent or more of their original price before the downturn. When the market recovers at whatever time, the club will benefit more greatly from the recovery than if they had kept those nonperforming stocks.

Again, limit yourself to sectors that are likely to be affected positively by the recovery—for instance, if the market decline was caused by cash crunch in the economy due to non-release of budgetary allocation. All you need do is to look at the sector highly favoured by the budget and take position because, once the recovery begins, there will likely be a jump in share prices in that sector.

Set Your Eyes on Regulatory Policies

It is quite important to set your gaze on changes in regulators' policies because it has been observed that certain policies or inconsistencies in policy can directly or indirectly cause a serious negative drift in the market; therefore, investors should be concerned about what the regulators are saying or doing to avoid getting caught in between.

Enlist the Service of a Broker

Every member in an investment club should be a researcher on a particular stock, but that doesn't mean that such a member can possibly pick a good share, especially since he or she may not see what happens daily on the trading floor like every broker does. As a result, every club, aside from opening an account with a stock brokerage firm, should have a stockbroker in that firm on their payroll to manage their funds—somebody they can relate with at all times and who can be given the authority to make certain decisions on their behalf. Occasionally, he or she should be invited to give investment tips and talk to members at meetings on financial matters.

8.4. Conclusion

The stock market, like other forms of investment, remains one of the channels for investing. Creation of wealth should not be ignored by any organisation that wishes to raise capital for growth and expansion activities rather than depend on subventions from government or donor agencies alone. Suffice it to say, organisations should not invest funds from donor organisations meant for particular projects in the capital market; instead, they should invest only what they have contributed as individual members towards wealth building. That way, when profit is made, a portion of it can be ploughed back as donation to the organisation's purse to boost funding of its activities.

It is also true that the capital market experiences its ups and downs, and that is why one should have a clear-cut objective before entering: so that one does not enter when he or she should be exiting. When the market nosedives for whatever reason, there is no doubt that during such a period most investors become despondent and jittery, but it takes a brave heart and a knowledgeable mind to continue to invest in growth stocks. In fact, when prices are at the lowest in a bear market that has good fundamentals and is about to rebound, this is the best period to buy more shares because prices of those shares with good fundamentals can never be bought cheaper, particularly when prices of such shares have reached their support level. Besides, limiting one's exposure to risk requires a lot of financial information about the company one is about to invest in. Beyond that, each investor must shun sentiments in choosing shares to invest in and conduct some basic research about the company to be invested in through financial publications, company reports, internet sources, market hearsay, etc.

Lastly, clubs must also be conscious of the fact that no group or individual becomes prosperous by stockpiling cash in their bank account.

OPIATES
Annual prevalence of abuse as percentage of the population aged
15-64 (unless otherwise indicated)

Southern Africa		Middle East and South-West Asia	
South Africa*, 2005	0.4	Iran, Islamic Republic, 1999	2.8
Zambia*, 2003	0.4	Afghanistan*, 2005	1.4
Dem.Republic of Congo, 2004	0.2	Pakistan*, 2000	0.7
Swaziland, 2004	0.2	Israel, (18-40), 2005	0.5
Zimbabwe, 2004	0.04	Bahrain, 1998	0.3
Namibia, 2000	0.03	Jordan*, 2001	0.2
West and Central Africa		Kuwait*, 2004	0.2
Nigeria*, (10+), 1999	0.6	Lebanon, 2003	0.2
Angola*, 2001	0.3	Oman, 1999	0.09
Chad, 1995	0.2	Yemen**, 1999	0.07
Liberia, 2004	0.2	Syrian Arab Rep.*, 2005	0.02
Sierra Leone, 1997	0.2	United Arab Emirates*, 2004	0.02
Central African Republic, 2004	0.1	Qatar, 1996	0.01
Congo Rep., 2004	0.1	Saudi Arabia, 2000	0.01
Ghana, 2004	0.1	**South Asia**	
Niger, 2004	0.1	Bangladesh*, 2003/4	0.4
Senegal**	0.03	India, 2001	0.4
Cote d'Ivoire, 1997	0.01	Nepal, 1996	0.3
ASIA		Sri Lanka*, 2004	0.1
Central Asia and Transcaucasia		Maldives**, 2001	0.2
Kazakhstan, 2006	1.0		
Kyrgyzstan, 2006	0.8		
Uzbekistan, 2006	0.8		
Georgia, 2000	0.6		
Tajikistan, 2006	0.5		
Armenia, 2005	0.3		
Turkmenistan**, 1998	0.3		
Azerbaijan, 2000	0.2		
East and South-East Asia			
Macao SAR, China, 2003	1.1		
Lao People's Dem. Rep., 2006	0.6		
Myanmar, 2006	0.6		
Taiwan province*, China, 2002	0.3		
Viet Nam, 2005	0.3		
China, 2003	0.2		
Hong Kong SAR, China, 2005	0.2		
Indonesia, 2005	0.2		
Malaysia*, 2000	0.2		
Thailand, 2006	0.1		
Japan¹, 2003	0.06		
Cambodia, 2004	0.03		
Brunei Darussalam, 1998	0.01		
Singapore*, 2004	0.01		

¹ Life-time prevalence (15+)

*UNODC estimates based on local studies, special population group studies, and/or
law enforcement agency assessments.
** Tentative estimates.
Sources: Annual Reports Questionnaires, Government Reports, US Department of
State, European Monitoring Center for Drugs and Drug Addiction (EMCDDA), Drug
Abuse Information Network for Asia and the Pacific (DAINAP), UNODC Global
Assessment Programme on Drug Abuse (GAP).

United Nations world drug report 2007

Table 14: Annual prevalence of amphetamines use, 2005 or latest year available

	Number of users	In per cent of population 15-64 years
EUROPE	2,750,000	0.5
West and Central Europe	2,220,000	0.7
South-East Europe	180,000	0.2
Eastern Europe	350,000	0.7
AMERICAS	5,710,000	1.0
North America	3,790,000	1.3
South America	1,920,000	0.7
ASIA	13,700,000	0.5
OCEANIA	620,000	2.9
AFRICA	2,100,000	0.4
GLOBAL	24,890,000	0.6

Above global average   Around global average   Below global average

United Nations world drug report 2007

Fig. 12: Annual prevalence of cannabis use, 2005 or latest year available

	No. of users	in % of population 15-64 years
EUROPE	30,500,000	5.6
West & Central Europe	23,400,000	7.4
South-East Europe	1,700,000	2.0
Eastern Europe	5,400,000	3.8
AMERICAS	37,600,000	6.5
North America	30,900,000	10.7
South America	6,700,000	2.3
ASIA	49,100,000	1.9
OCEANIA	3,400,000	15.8
AFRICA	38,200,000	7.7
GLOBAL	158,800,000	3.8

Above global average   Around global average   Below global average

United Nations world drug report 2007

3.5.2 Treatment demand (primary drugs of abuse)

3.5.2.1 Primary drugs of abuse among persons treated for drug problems in Africa

Country*	Source	Year	Distribution of main drugs in percentages								People treated**
			Cannabis	Opiates	Cocaine	Amphetamine-type stimulants	Methaqualone	Depressants	Inhalants	Khat	
Algeria	ARQ	1999/2004***	81.3%	6.6%	0.2%				2.1%		3,000
Botswana	SENDU	2003	100.0%								17
Burkina Faso	GAP	2005	80.0%	3.2%	4.7%			1.1%	4.4%		275
Cameroon(a)	RAS	1995	48.5%	12.1%	13.6%	43.6%			36.4%		16
Chad	ARQ	1996	50.6%	-	0.2%	18.8%			6.3%		41
Congo	ARQ	1995	100.0%								
Cote d'Ivoire	ARQ	1998	91.0%	4.1%	3.0%						
Egypt	UNODC FO	1999	22.1%	45.1%	0.4%						35
Ethiopia	ARQ	2005	8.6%	37.1%						54.3%	1,531
Ghana	GAP	2005	84.5%	0.4%	1.0%					11.4%	402
Kenya(b)	Univ.	2005	36.3%	37.8%	9.7%	0.5%		0.5%	1.2%		54
Lesotho	SENDU	2004	100.0%								342
Madagascar	ARQ	2005	100.0%								796
Malawi	SENDU	2004	100.0%								592
Mauritius	ARQ	2003	22.3%	58.3%	11.4%				0.5%		150
Mozambique	SENDU	2004	33.3%	54.7%	24.4%						41
Namibia	ARQ	2005	2.4%	2.4%	0.7%	9.8%	61.0%				925
Nigeria	Govt	2004	89.7%	1.2%	72.2%	2.0%		3.9%	3.7%		202
Sao Tome & Principe	ARQ	1997	22.2%	5.5%	2.0%						65
Senegal	GAP	2005	78.0%	1.0%		1.0%					2,067
Seychelles	ARQ	2005	55.4%	43.1%		1.5%			11.0%		14,741
Sierra Leone	ARQ	1997	96.8%		0.6%						128
South Africa	ARQ	2005	34.0%	10.8%	17.5%	18.3%	14.3%	5.2%			340
Swaziland	SENDU	2004	92.2%	0.9%	0.9%		4.7%	0.9%			162
Tanzania	SENDU	2004	62.7%	32.7%							233
Togo	ARQ	2002							34.6%		
Zambia	ARQ	2005	56.2%	4.3%	4.9%						
Total											26,155
Average			63.4%	14.5%	9.8%	11.9%	3.6%	0.5%	4.2%	3.0%	

* Please note that treatment definitions differ from country to country
.. Excluding alcohol.
... The second year specified is for the number of people treated (last column)
(a) Proxy: drugs totally consumed, based on key informants from social services (health affairs), from traditional healers, and repression.
(b) Proxy: cohort of abusers identified from rehabilitation centres, treatment centres, hospitals, streets, and drug dens within 5 urban areas.

Sources: UNODC, Annual Reports Questionnaires (ARQ); and Field Office (FO) data, Southern African Development Community (Epidemiology Network on Drug Use (SENDU), International Psychology Reporter).
UNODC Global Assessment Programme on Drug Abuse (GAP)

Table 6.   Annual prevalence of the use of cannabis, opioids and opiates, by region

Region or subregion	Cannabis Number (thousands)			Cannabis Prevalence (percentage)			Opioids Number (thousands)			Opioids Prevalence (percentage)			Opiates Number (thousands)			Opiates Prevalence (percentage)		
	Best estimate	Lower	Upper	Best estimate	Lower	Upper	Best estimate	Lower	Upper	Best estimate	Lower	Upper	Best estimate	Lower	Upper	Best estimate	Lower	Upper
Africa	44 960	21 840	57 340	7.8	3.8	10.0	2 200	930	3 840	0.4	0.2	0.7	2 110	880	3 280	0.4	0.2	0.6
East Africa	5 840	2 440	9 160	4.2	1.7	6.5	570	150	1 850	0.4	0.1	1.3	540	150	1 350	0.4	0.1	1.0
North Africa	7 530	4 790	10 600	5.7	3.6	8.0	330	130	540	0.3	0.1	0.4	330	130	540	0.3	0.1	0.4
Southern Africa	4 330	3 160	7 870	5.4	3.9	9.8	330	220	350	0.4	0.3	0.4	280	190	300	0.3	0.2	0.4
West and Central Africa	27 260	11 460	29 710	12.4	5.2	13.5	970	430	1 100	0.4	0.2	0.5	950	410	1 090	0.4	0.2	0.5
Americas	40 810	40 410	42 280	6.6	6.6	6.9	13 230	12 530	14 010	2.1	2.0	2.3	1 520	1 090	1 810	0.2	0.2	0.3
Caribbean	760	460	2 050	2.8	1.7	7.6	100	60	190	0.4	0.2	0.7	80	50	160	0.3	0.2	0.6
Central America	590	570	630	2.4	2.3	2.5	120	110	150	0.5	0.4	0.6	20	20	20	0.1	0.1	0.1
North America	32 950	32 950	32 950	10.8	10.8	10.8	12 180	11 580	12 790	4.0	3.8	4.2	1 310	920	1 500	0.4	0.3	0.5
South America	6 510	6 390	6 610	2.5	2.5	2.5	840	790	880	0.3	0.3	0.3	110	100	120	0.04	0.04	0.05
Asia	52 990	26 510	92 380	1.9	1.0	3.4	10 560	8 480	13 140	0.4	0.3	0.5	10 140	8 150	12 640	0.4	0.3	0.5
Central Asia	2 050	1 800	2 130	3.9	3.5	4.1	460	450	480	0.9	0.9	0.9	420	410	440	0.8	0.8	0.8
East and South-East Asia	9 710	5 720	22 560	0.6	0.4	1.5	4 370	3 500	5 650	0.3	0.2	0.4	4 310	3 410	5 580	0.3	0.2	0.4
Near and Middle East	8 140	2 360	15 840	3.1	0.9	6.1	2 900	2 410	3 490	1.1	0.9	1.3	2 700	2 240	3 310	1.0	0.9	1.3
South Asia	33 100	15 500	50 720	3.6	1.7	5.5	2 820	2 110	3 520	0.3	0.2	0.4	2 700	2 090	3 310	0.3	0.2	0.4
Europe	28 680	28 460	28 970	5.2	5.1	5.2	4 050	3 890	4 310	0.7	0.7	0.8	2 980	2 830	3 210	0.5	0.5	0.6
Eastern and South-Eastern Europe	6 150	5 990	6 400	2.7	2.6	2.6	2 810	2 800	2 900	1.2	1.2	1.3	1 870	1 860	1 960	0.8	0.8	0.8
Western and Central Europe	22 530	22 470	522 580	6.9	6.9	7.0	1 250	1 080	1 410	0.4	0.3	0.4	1 110	970	1 260	0.3	0.3	0.4
Oceania	2 630	2 200	3 520	10.9	9.1	14.6	730	550	820	3.0	2.3	3.4	40	40	60	0.2	0.2	0.2
Global estimate	170 070	119 420	224 490	3.8	2.6	5.0	30 780	26 380	36 120	0.7	0.6	0.8	16 790	12 980	20 990	0.4	0.3	0.5

United Nations world drug report 2012

Table 7. Annual prevalence of the use of cocaine, amphetamines and "ecstasy", by region

Region or subregion	Cocaine						ATS (excluding "ecstasy")						"Ecstasy"					
	Number (thousands)			Prevalence (percentage)			Number (thousands)			Prevalence (percentage)			Number (thousands)			Prevalence (percentage)		
	Best estimate	Lower	Upper	Best estimate	Lower	Upper	Best estimate	Lower	Upper	Best estimate	Lower	Upper	Best estimate	Lower	Upper	Best estimate	Lower	Upper
Africa	**2 780**	**950**	**4 610**	**0.5**	**0.2**	**0.8**	**4 730**	**1 190**	**8 270**	**0.8**	**0.2**	**1.4**	**1 160**	**400**	**1 930**	**0.2**	**0.1**	**0.3**
East Africa	:	:	:	:	:	:	:	:	:	:	:	:	:	:	:	:	:	:
North Africa	40	30	50	0.03	0.03	0.04	:	:	:	:	:	:	:	:	:	:	:	:
Southern Africa	630	270	850	0.8	0.3	1.1	590	290	790	0.7	0.4	1.0	300	190	300	0.4	0.2	0.4
West and Central Africa	1 530	560	2 330	0.7	0.3	1.1	:	:	:	:	:	:	:	:	:	:	:	:
Americas	**7 150**	**6 990**	**7 380**	**1.2**	**1.1**	**1.2**	**5 790**	**5 450**	**6 550**	**0.9**	**0.9**	**1.1**	**3 230**	**3 160**	**3 400**	**0.5**	**0.5**	**0.6**
Caribbean	180	110	330	0.7	0.4	1.2	220	30	530	0.8	0.1	1.9	80	10	240	0.3	0.1	0.9
Central America	130	130	140	0.5	0.5	0.6	330	330	330	1.3	1.3	1.3	30	20	30	0.1	0.1	0.1
North America	5 000	5 000	5 000	1.6	1.6	1.6	3 920	3 920	3 920	1.3	1.3	1.3	2 710	2 710	2 710	0.9	0.9	0.9
South America	1 840	1 760	1 910	0.7	0.7	0.7	1 310	1 170	1 770	0.5	0.4	0.7	420	420	420	0.2	0.2	0.2
Asia	**1 270**	**400**	**2 200**	**0.05**	**0.01**	**0.08**	**19 570**	**4 943**	**34 201**	**0.7**	**0.2**	**1.2**	**10 380**	**2 580**	**18 180**	**0.4**	**0.1**	**0.7**
Central Asia	:	:	:	:	:	:	:	:	:	:	:	:	:	:	:	:	:	:
East and South-East Asia	420	310	1 070	0.03	0.02	0.07	8 400	3 740	19 510	0.6	0.2	1.3	2 820	1 590	6 380	0.2	0.1	0.4
Near and Middle East	70	50	120	0.03	0.02	0.05	570	310	1 260	0.2	0.1	0.5	:	:	:	:	:	:
South Asia	:	:	:	:	:	:	:	:	:	:	:	:	:	:	:	:	:	:
Europe	**4 650**	**4 490**	**4 870**	**0.8**	**0.8**	**0.9**	**2 640**	**2 350**	**2 950**	**0.5**	**0.4**	**0.5**	**3 740**	**3 650**	**3 900**	**0.7**	**0.7**	**0.7**
Eastern and South-Eastern Europe	480	320	670	0.2	0.1	0.3	780	510	1 060	0.3	0.2	0.5	1 280	1 210	1 390	0.6	0.5	0.6
Western and Central Europe	4 160	4 170	4 200	1.3	1.3	1.3	1 870	1 840	1 900	0.6	0.6	0.6	2 460	2 440	2 510	0.8	0.8	0.8
Oceania	**370**	**370**	**450**	**1.5**	**1.5**	**1.9**	**510**	**410**	**570**	**2.1**	**1.7**	**2.4**	**710**	**690**	**710**	**2.9**	**2.9**	**2.9**
Global estimate	**16 220**	**13 200**	**19 510**	**0.4**	**0.3**	**0.4**	**33 240**	**14 343**	**52 541**	**0.7**	**0.3**	**1.2**	**19 220**	**10 480**	**28 120**	**0.4**	**0.2**	**0.6**

United Nations world drug report 2012

Bibliography

Books, Articles, and Journals

ACTION, a journal published by the Lagos State AIDS Control Agency (LSACA), 2008.

Agbonlahor, F. I. and A. O. Olutayo. *Issues and Perspectives in Sociology*. Benin: 1995

Audu, Hauwa M. *Can Every Nigerian Be a Millionaire?* Lagos: Amyn Investments Ltd., 2005.

Barber, James G. *Social Work with Addictions*, 2nd ed. New York: Palgrave Macmillan, 2002.

Boyte, Harry, and Nancy N. Kari. "Renewing the Democratic Spirit in American Colleges and Universities: Higher Education as Public Work." *Higher Education and Civic Responsibility,* 1999.

Brown, Carolyn M. *The Millionaires' Club*. New York: John Wiley & Sons, 2000.

Calvert, Susan, and Peter Calvert. *Sociology Today*. Hertfordshire: Harvester Wheatsheaf, 1992.

Cohen, Bernice. *The Armchair Investor*. London: Orion Publishers, 1997.

———. *The Wealthy Investor*. London: Orion Publishers, 2000.

Constitution of the Federal Republic of Nigeria, 1999.

David, Joe C. *Be Your Own Boss*. Lagos: Perdec Associates, 2003.

Dominelli, Lena. *Sociology for Social Work*. London: Macmillan, 1997.

Dominic, Matthew O. *Effect of Substance Abuse among Youths: A Nigerian Perspective*. Paper presentation accepted for the 14th International Conference of the Association of Psychology & Psychiatry for Adults & Children (A.P.P.A.C), Greece, May 2009.

Dorch, Patricia. "17 Essential Strategies for Networking in the 21st Century," www.selfgrowth.com/articles/Dorch1.html, 2008.

"Drug Use Report by Women in Society on Homeless Youths in Melbourne and Los Angeles," 2003.

Edwards, Griffith. *Matters of Substance*, 2nd ed. New York: Penguin Books, 2005.

Elsdon, K. T., with John Reynolds and Susan Stewart. *Voluntary Organizations: Citizenship, Learning, and Change*. National Institute of Adult Learning & Department of Adult Education. London: University of Nottingham, 1995.

Engel, Louise, and Brendan Engel. *How to Buy Stocks*, 7th ed. New York: Bantam Books, 1982.

Ewemie, Ben. *Essentials of Citizenship Education in Nigeria*. Benin: Joeseg Associates, 2000.

Gbede, G. Omotayo. *Cyber Marketing*. Lagos: Westbourne Business School, 2002.

Ghodse, Hamid. *Drugs and Addictive Behaviour: A Guide to Treatment*. London: Blackwell Science Publishers, 1995.

The Good News Bible: Today's English Version. Lagos: St Paul's Publication, 1994.

Gough, Leo. *Savings and Investment*. London: Hodder & Stoughton Educational Publishers, 1996.

Haralambos, Michael, Martin Holborn, and Robin Hald. *Sociology: Themes and Perspectives*, 5th ed. London: Collins Educational, 2000.

Hogg, Michael A., and Graham M. Vaughan. *Social Psychology*, 4th ed. Upper Saddle River, NJ: Pearson Education, 2005.

Jones, Gill, and Claire Wallace. *Youth, Family and Citizenship*. Buckingham: Open University Press, 1992.

Klein, Axel. *Drugs and the World*. London: Reaktion Books Ltd, 2008.

Lawson, Tony, and Tim Heaton. *Crime and Deviance*. New York: Palgrave Macmillan, 1999.

Mills, Steven. *Youth Lifestyles in a Changing World*. Buckingham: Open University Press, 2000.

National Youth Policy of the Federal Republic of Nigeria, 2001.

Newman, Bill. *Soaring with Eagles: Principles of Success*. Bill Newman International, 1997.

O'Donnell, Mike. *Introduction to Sociology*. London: Thomas Nelson & Sons Ltd, 1997.

United Nations Office of Drugs & Crime: World Drug Report 2007 published by UN, New York, 2007.

Vintcent, Charles. *Be Your Own Stockbroker*. Pitman Publishing, 1997.

Willocks, Sarah. "Social Work with Children & Families" course notes. London: Stonebridge Associated Colleges, 2008.

Worsley, P. *Introducing Sociology*, 3rd ed. London: Penguin Books, 1987.

Internet Resources

www.publicwork.org/articles

www.biznik.com/articles

http://bizcovering.com/investing/investing-in-a-nigerian-
bear-market-strategies-to-adopt/

www.ezinearticles.com

www.who.int

www.unodc.org/unodc/en/data-and-analysis/WDR-2011.
html

www.ingramcontent.com/pod-product-compliance
Lightning Source LLC
Chambersburg PA
CBHW020519290526
45786CB00002B/679